The Spiritual Solution
SIMPLE AND EFFECTIVE RECOVERY THROUGH THE TAKING AND TEACHING OF THE 12 STEPS

John H

SIMPLE ENLIGHTENMENT PRESS

Contact, Workshops and blog information:
www.johnh12steps.com
www.thespiritualsolution.org

ssbook@johnh12steps.com
johnh12steps@gmail.com

Additional copies of this book are available from Amazon.com and other distributors. For more information, please contact Simple Enlightenment Press through the sites above.

This book is not meant to be a substitute for the book Alcoholics Anonymous. There is much additional material in The Big Book that is very beneficial to all alcoholics.

Dedication

This book is dedicated to my parents, Josephine and Andrew, gentle and loving souls who, despite my behavior, made certain I always knew I was loved.

And to my partner Moira, a gentle and loving soul herself who has taught me the way of patience, tolerance, kindness and love. I hope I have always shown her that she is loved.

Contents

Part 1 Introduction

Part 2 The Spiritual Solution Workshop

Part 3 Practicing These Principles

Acknowledgements

The Spiritual Solution workshops would never have happened without the support and skillful suggestions of my partner, Moira K. This book would not have been possible without your love and support and your insightful and sober contributions. Thank you for everything, and most importantly, for helping me stay sober day by day.

To Jim K: Despite my protestations, you intuitively knew how to handle my situation. Thank you.

To Dan L who reached out his hand to me when it felt like no one would. Thank you.

To all the men who made me a part of their sobriety by blessing me as their sponsor: Ryan T, Brian L, Johnny G, JJ, Eddy B, John S, Greg M, Chris B, Don D, Mike H, Pam S, Brett P, Joe D, Chris P, Chris G, Chris V, Bill H, Jaime, Peter B, Danny, Joe D and many others over the years, you have all helped me stay sober a day at a time. Thank you.

To all the men and women who have attended (or will attend) The Spiritual Solution Workshops, you have all helped me stay sober. Thank You.

To al the members of my home groups, Sergeantsville 12/164, Milford 12/164 and the Reigelsville Surprise group, you have all helped me stay sober. Thank you.

To all the sober men and women of AA who have blessed me with their love and service. We need each other. Thank you.

To Bill Wilson and Dr. Bob Smith. Thank you for your willingness and courage to speak the truth and share your recovery with others. None of us would be here today without your love and service.

ACKNOWLEDGEMENTS

Finally, to the God of my understanding. Due to the spiritual solution to my alcoholism, and the brilliant AA principle of seeking "a God of my understanding" and knowing that I must continue to "grow along spiritual lines," my relationship with my higher power has evolved from a necessary dependence to an external power greater than my self, to an inner knowing that a power greater than my ego self is my true self, my own essential nature.

As Jesus said "seek ye first the kingdom of heaven within, and all great things will be added to you". In Dzogchen, the Dharmakaya, the inner body of truth, I have learned that "The essence of all phenomena is the awakened mind; the mind of all Buddha's is the awakened mind; and the life-force of all sentient beings is the awakened mind, too."

Without the great freedom to seek the God of my understanding, and the simple and direct path given to me to walk, a day at a time, I would never have experienced a sober day, and I would never have experienced who I truly am.

~~~

I also wish to express my deep gratitude to Tanja Butalovic for her great care and skill in editing the manuscript for this book. Thank you. Her wonderful blog is at www.bellyheartsoul.com

~~~

Part 1
Introduction

12 Steps Quick Guide

The 12 Steps as presented in The Big Book

Page and paragraph in this book in brackets [page:paragraph]
and from The Big Book in parentheses (page:paragraph)

Step 1: "We learned that we had to fully concede to our innermost selves that we were alcoholics. This is the first step in recovery." [51:4] (30:2)

Step 2: "Do I now believe, or am I even willing to believe, that there is a Power greater than myself?" [58:2] (47:2)

Step 3: "God, I offer myself to Thee - to build with me and to do with me as Thou wilt. Relieve me of the bondage of self, that I may better do Thy will. Take away my difficulties, that victory over them may bear witness to those I would help of Thy Power, Thy Love, and Thy Way of life. May I do Thy will always!" [66:1] (63:2)

Step 4: "Therefore, we started upon a personal inventory. This was *Step Four*." [73:3] (64:1)
(Inventory definition is "a detailed LIST")

Step 5: "...when completed, will mean that we have admitted to God, to ourselves, and to another human being, the exact nature of our defects." [77:1] (72:1)

Step 6: "Are we now ready to let God remove from us all the things which we have admitted are objectionable?" [91:2] (76:1)

Step 7: "My Creator, I am now willing that you should have all of me, good and bad. I pray that you now remove from me every single defect of character which stands in the way of my usefulness to you and my fellows. Grant me strength, as I go out from here, to do your bidding. Amen." [93:1] (76:2)

2

Step 8: "We have a list of all persons we have harmed and to whom we are willing to make amends. We made it when we took inventory." [95:2] (76:3)

Step 9: "Now we go out to our fellows and repair the damage done in the past. We attempt to sweep away the debris which has accumulated out of our effort to live on self-will and run the show ourselves." [97:1] (76:3)

Step 10: "This thought brings us to *Step Ten*, which suggests we continue to take personal inventory and continue to set right any new mistakes as we go along." [107:2] (84:2)

Step 11: "*Step Eleven* suggests prayer and meditation." (more) [111:1] (85:3)

(Big Book Page 85, Paragraph 3 Through Big Book Page 87, Paragraph 3)

Step 12: "Practical experience shows that nothing will so much insure **immunity from drinking** as intensive work with other alcoholics. It works when other activities fail. This is our *twelfth suggestion*: Carry this message to other alcoholics! You can help when no one else can. You can secure their confidence when others fail. Remember they are very ill." [115:1] (89:1)

The Founding of Alcoholics Anonymous and The Development of The Spiritual Solution to Alcoholism

An alcoholic in 1935 had very little hope of finding any effective treatment for their alcoholism. The overwhelming majority of alcoholics spent much of their lives in hospitals, jails, and mental institutions. They all faced a premature death. The medical community and the general public viewed alcoholics as hopelessly weak-willed and mentally defective.

Bill Wilson was once a wizard of Wall Street. By 1935, he was also an alcoholic of the hopeless variety. Bill had many stays in hospitals and had lost almost everything a person could lose due to his alcoholism. One day he was visited by an old friend and drinking partner, Ebby Thacher. Ebby, after a commitment to an asylum for the mentally ill alcoholic, was now sober for two months. Ebby's life turned when two men asked a judge to release Ebby to them on the condition that they would be responsible for him. These two men convinced Ebby that by incorporating spiritual principles into his life, including service to others, Ebby could stay sober.

Ebby visited Bill that day to explain to him how this spiritual solution to alcoholism transformed him, and how he thought that should Bill follow these same spiritual principles, it may work for him as well. Bill listened, skeptically at first, and as Ebby talked of a higher power, Bill recalled times in his own life when a higher power was significant to him. The next day, Bill entered a hospital as he showed signs of delirium tremens, a possibly fatal response to withdrawal from alcohol.

Ebby visited Bill again at the hospital, as Bill continued detoxification from the effects of many years of alcoholism. While there, Ebby further explained the spiritual solution he had used to overcome alcoholism. He explained to Bill the need to surrender to a higher power of Bill's own understanding. In order to deepen this surrender and further cultivate an understanding of a higher power, Ebby impressed on Bill the need to take an honest assessment of his behavior and how his behavior had caused others harm. He told Bill that he needed to make restitution, to set right harms done to others. He then explained to Bill that he must incorporate a spiritual practice into his daily life to maintain this new God-consciousness and to keep himself in fit spiritual condition, if Bill is to overcome alcoholism.

Most importantly, Ebby impressed on Bill the importance of practicing these spiritual principles in all of his affairs, and the absolute necessity of helping others. Soon after Ebby's visit, Bill had a spiritual experience where he felt renewed, and his thoughts changed from being self-centered to other-centered. While lying in his hospital bed, Bill understood how important it would be to help other alcoholics, as Ebby had helped him. He realized that if he helped others, they in turn could help others, and many thousands might be saved by following these simple spiritual principles.

Bill left the hospital with the conviction of being of service to other alcoholics. At first, Bill was not successful in helping alcoholics achieve the sobriety he had. One particularly troubling day for Bill, he arrived home despondent at his lack of success. He complained to his wife Lois that he had talked to hundreds of alcoholics, and that he was not able to help any of them. Lois' very significant reply was "Yes Bill, but you stayed sober!" For the first time in decades, by practicing these new-found spiritual principles, and by attempting to help other alcoholics, Bill could stay sober.

Soon after, Bill would have his first success. On a business trip to Akron, Ohio, he found himself in a hotel lobby. Bill

6

noticed the hotel bar and the happy patrons drinking inside. Bill, now six months sober, suddenly felt a compulsion to drink. He knew that he had to find another alcoholic to help or that he would most likely drink again. Desperately, Bill began calling churches and other organizations in the area, hoping someone could direct him to a drunk. On his nineteenth call he reached Henrietta Sieberling, who knew of a prime candidate.

However, Doctor Bob Smith, a once prominent local Doctor, was too drunk to see Bill that day. Nonetheless, for Bill, simply reaching out and trying to find an alcoholic to help was enough to change Bill's self-centered thinking, and he was able to   get through the day sober. The next day, Henrietta once again called Dr. Bob, who albeit reluctantly, agreed to meet Bill.

They talked for many hours, Bill explaining to his new friend Bob that he was once as hopeless as Bob was then. Bill further explained that he was able finally to stay sober by incorporating spiritual principles into his life and by helping other alcoholics. Dr. Bob was so impressed by Bill and the message he carried that he stopped drinking.

Bill stayed in Akron for business and continued to look for drunks he could work with. In the meantime, Bob traveled to Atlantic City for a business convention. While away, Dr. Bob drank again, eventually making it back to a town near Akron. Anne Smith, Dr. Bob's wife, received a call from a friend whose house Bob was staying at. Anne sent Bill to pick up Bob. They talked again about the need for a spiritual solution to Bob's alcoholism, including the need to help other alcoholics. Bill offered Dr. Bob a few more drinks that night, and one beer the next morning. Bob immediately incorporated the spiritual principles that Bill presented to him. Bob never drank alcohol again.

Bill's meeting with Bob is recognized as the birth of Alcoholics Anonymous: One alcoholic explaining to another alcoholic that any alcoholic could stay sober by transforming an extremely self-centered view of the world through the use of spiritual principles, including service to others. Although Bill and Bobs' success was slow at first, eventually small groups formed in Akron and New York. The most successful groups were the groups that incorporated the same spiritual ideals that Bill and Bob found most effective.

In order to reach more alcoholics and to explain the spiritual solution to alcoholism, Bill, Bob, and approximately 100 other early AA members decided to write and publish a book.

The First Edition of Alcoholics Anonymous was published in 1939. With the publishing of Alcoholics Anonymous, commonly known as The Big Book, alcoholics everywhere would be able to understand the spiritual approach to treating alcoholism. The message of recovery began to get attention in other ways, including newspaper and magazine articles. By the printing of the Second Edition of The Big Book in 1955, an estimated 150,000 alcoholics achieved sobriety by using the spiritual principles of Alcoholics Anonymous. At the time of the Third Edition publication in 1976, membership in AA reached approximately two million people. Today, in 2012, there are still an estimated two million AA members.

The First Edition of Alcoholics Anonymous, clearly and simply explained the spiritual solution for alcoholism that Bill Wilson, Dr. Bob Smith, and other early members relied on for their sobriety, and for helping other alcoholics. These spiritual principles are understood by taking the 12 steps as presented in The Big book. Taking others through the 12 steps deepens our understanding of these spiritual principles. By doing this, we are able to overcome the often fatal self-centeredness common to alcoholics. This is the only suggested program of recovery that Alcoholics Anonymous has to offer.

Since the founding of Alcoholics Anonymous, there has been continuous debate within AA as to the necessity of the spiritual solution to alcoholism. Some early members objected strongly to the spiritual nature of AA and the guidance towards the need for surrender, personal inventory, conscious contact with a higher power, and service to others. Those opposed to a spiritual solution to alcoholism thought that drinking could be avoided just by meeting with other alcoholics using peer pressure and engaging in individual problem resolution.

Members who had gained sobriety through the 12 Steps, including service to others, insisted that AA was founded on spiritual principles and that the success of AA was due to alcoholics following the direction of the founders and other early members.

This early debate regarding the spiritual nature of Alcoholics Anonymous led to concessions in the presentation of what exactly constitutes the AA Program of recovery. Even though there existed no other defined spiritual program of recovery other than The Twelve Steps, the internal pressure from some members who had stayed sober for a time despite their rejection of the spiritual principles of recovery, caused the wording of the introduction to The Twelve Steps in The Big Book to read:

"Here are the steps we took which are **suggested** as a program of recovery."

The words to "How It Works" describe precisely the spiritual solution to alcoholism. "How It Works" is read at the beginning of most AA meetings. Despite the clear direction that AA is a spiritual solution to alcoholism (found in the taking and teaching of the 12 Steps), the ambiguity in wording by reducing the importance of the spiritual solution to alcoholism to a mere suggestion has had unintended consequences. A fellowship founded on spiritual principles 77 years ago, has many AA members today rejecting the spirituality of the 12 step program of recovery deeming it optional and unnecessary.

By reducing the importance in taking the 12 Steps to a mere suggestion, the effectiveness in actually relieving the suffering of all alcoholics has been greatly diminished.

Due to the structure of AA, defined loosely by a set of Twelve Traditions, often misinterpreted, no member of AA is compelled to do anything or believe in any way. In this sense, the spiritual solution to alcoholism, the only suggested program of recovery, has certainly become optional. By not defining exactly what should be done to achieve the spiritual solution to alcoholism, by making the spiritual solution a mere suggestion, many alcoholics decide to either ignore the spiritual solution entirely, or change it to fit their own view of "How It Works".

The clear, simple, straightforward directions for taking the 12 Steps found in The Big Book have been added to and embellished in many different ways. This has made the 12 Steps much more complicated and much less effective, which in turn has led alcoholics, especially newcomers, to avoid or disregard the only suggested program of recovery.

By delaying or disregarding the example, leadership and suggestions of our founders, what was once a very successful spiritual treatment for alcoholism, at one time documenting a 50% to 60% recovery rate, can now only claim a 5% to 7% recovery rate.

(In 1990, AA GSO, the governing organization overseeing all "autonomous" meetings, published an internal memo for the employees of its corporate offices. It was an analysis of a survey period between 1977 and 1989. "After just one month in the Fellowship [meaning AA,] 81% of the new members had already dropped out. After three months, 90% have left, and a full 95% have disappeared inside one year!") (Kolenda, 2003, Golden Text Publishing Company)

As stated previously, there has been no growth in the overall membership in Alcoholics Anonymous in over thirty years. As alcoholics have substituted other less effective or ineffective methods of staying sober in AA, the membership of AA has stagnated. Many members and even entire AA groups are outwardly hostile to any mention of a higher power, spirituality, or the 12 Steps. What was once a vibrant, effective and vital fellowship of men and women achieving and maintaining sobriety based on spiritual principles, is now an organization that has lost much of its original enthusiasm, focus and direction.

Today, it is the minority of members who actually follow the example of our founders by taking the 12 Steps as described in The Big Book, and then guide others through taking the steps in the same manner.

AA members who understand that those in a 12 step program should actually take and teach the 12 steps, are often shunned and dismissed by those members who reject the basic principles of AA.

To non-alcoholics reading this book, I hope it will help clarify for you a very effective treatment for alcoholism for anyone you may know that is in need of help with this devastating disease.

To alcoholics in AA or those still seeking a way out of their suffering, I hope that this book will help clarify for you the only suggested program of recovery that AA has to offer.

John H
February 29, 2012

The Spiritual Solution To Alcoholism

"To show other alcoholics PRECISELY HOW WE HAVE RECOVERED is the main purpose of this book." - from the Forward to the First Edition of Alcoholics Anonymous, commonly known as The Big Book.

"Further on, CLEAR-CUT DIRECTIONS are given showing HOW WE RECOVERED." - From page 29, paragraph 1, Alcoholics Anonymous.

"We needed to ask ourselves but one short question. 'Do I now believe, or am I even willing to believe, that there is a Power greater than myself?' As soon as a man can say that he does believe, or is willing to believe, we emphatically assure him that he is on his way. It has been repeatedly proven among us that upon this simple cornerstone a wonderfully effective spiritual structure can be built." - From page 47, paragraph 2, Alcoholics Anonymous.

My Name is John H and I am a member of Alcoholics Anonymous. There is significant misunderstanding of the fellowship of Alcoholics Anonymous and how the AA 12 Step spiritual solution to alcoholism actually helps alcoholics achieve sobriety. This misunderstanding and confusion is commonplace within the medical community and treatment facilities, and in the general population. Unfortunately, this misunderstanding and confusion is also commonplace within AA as well.

AA is not a secret organization nor are we ashamed of our disease. AA is not a cult. No one is coerced into believing any particular way or to follow or worship any individual or ideal. AA is not therapy in any conventional meaning. AA is a

13

fellowship of men and women who seek a spiritual solution to alcoholism. Once we have achieved the spiritual solution presented in our textbook, Alcoholics Anonymous, we stay sober by guiding other alcoholics to the same spiritual solution. The principles of AA and the only suggested program of recovery have not changed since our founding in 1935.

Although Alcoholics Anonymous was certainly influenced by Christian principles, AA is not affiliated with any organized religion and is free of any particular religious dogma.

The perception of many people, both inside and outside AA, is that AA is a quasi-religious organization, which uses peer pressure and group talk therapy to help alcoholics not drink. While certainly not the intention of our founders, Bill Wilson and Dr. Bob Smith, this is partly true today. As we have taken on other often ineffective methods of recovery, only loosely based on the 12 Steps as described in the book Alcoholics Anonymous, AA has lost its focus and effectiveness as a spiritual solution to alcoholism.

Many alcoholics who consider themselves members of AA reject the founding principle of AA as a spiritual solution to alcoholism achieved by taking and teaching the 12 Steps.

AA was founded on spiritual principles including love, tolerance, compassion, honesty, conscious contact with a power greater than human power, and service to others. As AA became sidetracked from its singleness of purpose of providing a spiritual solution to alcoholism based on these principles, it has lost much of its effectiveness.

Today, many alcoholics come to AA from treatment centers. As the proliferation of treatment centers has grown, numerous AA groups have incorporated the therapeutic model of group therapy, extensive self-analysis, and behavior modification into their meetings. This type of therapy is entirely appropriate in a therapeutic setting. It has also been a considerable detriment to the intended spiritual setting of Alcoholics Anonymous.

~~~

This book includes The Spiritual Solution One-Day 12 Step Workshop, and has been written to show where AA has become diverted from its singleness of purpose, and how the spiritual solution to alcoholism (and other addictions) is just as effective today as it was 77 years ago.

It is important to note that all the positive aspects of AA lead to a very supportive fellowship. The various suggestions and slogans and the many ways that members of AA are of service to each other and all of AA, contribute greatly to the well-being of all alcoholics. It is very important to keep in mind that being of service, attending 90 meetings in 90 days, practicing slogans, etc., while helpful, are not a substitute for taking and teaching the 12 Steps.

We are all responsible for the effectiveness of AA, and the message of recovery presented in AA. We are all part of a once highly successful program, which today has very limited success in presenting the spiritual solution to alcoholism.

It is my intention in writing this book to point out where we have lost focus by not following the original intention of our founders, and to provide a guide to the simple directions for recovery presented in the Alcoholics Anonymous book. The Spiritual Solution Workshops provide a simple, effective and straightforward method for those suffering with alcoholism and other substance abuse issues to take all 12 Steps in one sitting as they are presented in The Big Book. A typical Spiritual Solution workshop lasts approximately six hours with a break midway.

The only suggested program of recovery presented in the book Alcoholics Anonymous is the 12 Steps. By taking all 12 Steps as presented in the AA textbook, an alcoholic has a direct experience of the spiritual solution to alcoholism.

Many alcoholics taking the steps today do so in a very protracted and complicated manner that is not nearly as effective as the simple and direct way described in The Big Book.

Nowhere in The Big Book can one find instructions to

study the steps, work the steps, or analyze the steps. We are not looking for an individual meaning to the steps or an individual interpretation of the steps.

Recovery through the 12 Steps is not an intellectual or psychological exercise. The 12 Steps are not more effective by "working the steps" during a 12 week or 12 month Big Book course of study. These methods will often confuse and delay or prevent the spiritual solution. Recovery in AA was never meant to be treated as an elective college course.

By taking all 12 Steps in one sitting the momentum and spiritual connection established is maintained and strengthened from one step to the next.

Deconstructing The Big Book searching for every use of the word "should" or "must," or how many references there are to God, a higher power, or any other study or analysis of The Big Book is only counter-productive, especially for the one who requires a simple and effective way to the spiritual solution, the still sick and suffering newcomer. These other methods make a simple and straightforward program of recovery more complicated and much less effective, and often impossible to understand.

The result of this complication and embellishment of the steps is that many in AA today feel that the steps are not to be taken in early sobriety, if at all.

Many who come to AA do not take the steps due to the complicated nature in which the steps are presented. Many who do actually take the steps using other methods become confused and discouraged when they begin, or soon afterward. Some members who have never taken the steps, or have taken the steps in a manner they were never intended to be taken, spread much fear and confusion about a very simple program of recovery.

Newcomers, still suffering the effects of active alcoholism, are told to go off by themselves and to analyze and write down every experience of powerlessness and unmanageability in their entire lives just to take   step one. They are then told to

16

meet with their sponsors and re-analyze all these incidences of powerlessness and unmanageability. Once the sponsor decides that this new member has done a sufficient amount of work, study, and confusing and distracting analysis, the sponsor declares that they have completed step 1.

More often than not, both the sponsor and sponsee become so distracted by these embellishments to a simple question and answer, that the newcomer never actually takes step 1. Then over the next weeks, months, or even years, this method of "working" the steps is repeated until the sponsee becomes so discouraged they quit "step work" altogether. Those who actually "work" their way through all 12 Steps often know nothing more about the spiritual solution to their alcoholism than when they first came to AA.

The sponsee is then left wondering why, after so much complicated work and study, they are yet to experience the complete psychic change and spiritual awakening promised to those that actually take the steps. They do not understand why they are still restless, irritable and discontented. They will often blame themselves believing that they simply did not put enough effort into the "work" or that they are not capable of understanding a (now) very complicated process. Many will drink again and blame AA without ever being offered the only suggested program of recovery. If they do stay sober and continue in AA, they then carry the same confusing and complicated method to their own sponsees because it was taught to them in this manner.

All that is needed to take the steps as they are presented is an honest desire to stop drinking and a willingness to follow the simple directions in The Big Book.

The steps in The Big Book are very easy to follow. They are presented in a clear and direct way so that the suffering AA newcomer can take all 12 Steps and within a few hours, experience a complete psychic change and spiritual awakening. Once this change has taken place, they begin immediately to help other alcoholics. We help others not only as a result of taking the 12 Steps, we help others as a continuation of spiritual growth and maintenance of our own sobriety.

This is how our co-founders Bill Wilson and Dr. Bob Smith recovered, and it is precisely the program of recovery that is presented here.

By establishing in newcomers the awareness that once they have taken the steps as presented in The Big Book, they have now fit themselves to help other alcoholics in the same way. The newcomer now has the confidence to begin to practice these new-found spiritual principles. By helping other alcoholics, the newcomer immediately gains a strong sense of purpose and quickly begins to overcome the extreme self-centeredness so characteristic of the alcoholic.

Once this is accomplished, the newcomer is well on their way to comfortable contented sobriety in service to others. As important, by following this method, the newcomer avoids years of grim and tenuous sobriety, the dry drunk syndrome many alcoholics experience by rejecting the spiritual solution and merely not drinking and going to meetings.

Is there any reason that any alcoholic should be told to wait for their recovery? Only a complete misunderstanding of the AA spiritual solution to alcoholism could lead to this misguided advice. The steps are to be taken as soon as one comes to AA. In the early days, when AA had a much higher recovery rate, established AA members often took newcomers through the steps while the newcomers were still detoxing in hospitals.

Those that have been through the steps using other methods, some encompassing pages and pages of writing and months and months of dialog, (believing that they are taking the steps as they were designed), often have a difficult time accepting that one can actually take all 12 Steps in one sitting lasting five or six hours.

Experience and the Big Book prove differently. The Big Book is written in a straightforward way and the directions are clear as to how the steps are to be taken. The Spiritual Solution

Workshop guidelines provide a simple and effective method of taking all 12 Steps as they are presented in our textbook, Alcoholics Anonymous.

A perfect example of how the steps as presented in The Big Book are simple and straightforward is the explanation of the first two steps we read at most every meeting. At the end of "How It Works" The Big Book authors state:

> "Our description of the alcoholic, the chapter to the agnostic, and our personal adventures before and after make clear three pertinent ideas:
>
> (a) That we were alcoholic and could not manage our own lives.
> (b) That probably no human power could have relieved our alcoholism.
> (c) That God could and would if He were sought."

The next line in The Big Book, often omitted during the reading of "How It Works", states:

> "Being convinced, *we were at Step Three*, which is that we decided to turn our will and our life over to God as we understood Him."

Once we become convinced we are alcoholic, that we need a higher or greater than human power to relieve our alcoholism, and that we believe in or were willing to believe in a higher or greater power than human power, we have taken the first two steps.

On page 30, paragraph 2 of The Big Book the authors are even more clear regarding what is required to take steps 1 and 2:

> **"We learned that he had to fully concede to our innermost selves that we were alcoholics. This is the first step in recovery. "**

On page 47 paragraph 2, the authors write:

"We needed to ask ourselves but one short question. Do I now believe, or am I even willing to believe, that there is a Power greater than myself? As soon as a man can say that he does believe, or is willing to believe, we emphatically assure him that he is on his way."

Steps 1 and 2 are simply an acknowledgment of the problem, alcoholism, and an affirmative answer to the question: **Do I now believe in a power greater than myself, and if not, am I willing to change my mind about a higher power?**

As can be seen, there is no writing involved in taking steps 1 or 2. The only steps in which we are instructed to do any writing are (the simple) step 4 and step 10 inventory lists. There are no instructions to perform an endless analysis of every incidence of powerlessness or unmanageability or philosophical or psychological exploration of the meaning of God or other simple concepts such as willingness, honesty or selfishness. There are no instructions for writing our life story or drunk-a-log.

We are not instructed to create multi-page worksheets in order to take a simple fourth step inventory, nor are we instructed to write endlessly, searching for a deeper or hidden meaning in the steps, or for some obscure bit of our past that we could point to as the cause of our alcoholism.

"Selfishness – self-centeredness! That we think is the root of our troubles." (Big Book, page 62, paragraph 1)

Self-centeredness is the defining characteristic of the alcoholic. Through the simple inventory process described in The Big Book, and used in The Spiritual Solution Workshop, we are provided with the tools to identify all the common manifestations of self-centeredness and gain the help of a power greater than our ego selves to finally be free of them.

Self-centered thinking, intensified in the minds of many

alcoholics, though hardly ever recognized by the alcoholic, is what causes the "compulsion of the mind", which coupled with an "allergy of the body", leads to active alcoholism. This same selfish view of life, if left untreated, often will lead to a self-centered compulsion of focusing on individual problems even while staying sober.

Using the simple fourth step list described in The Big Book, we quickly learn to identify all the manifestations of self-centeredness and then in prayer and meditation, seek a higher or greater power's help in removing these self-centered defects of character. We are not instructed to use dialog (human power) to remove our character defects, only to identify them. It is through conscious contact with a higher power that the alcoholic gains relief from self-centeredness.

By using a simple checklist, as instructed, we do not get hopelessly bogged down and distracted with every minute detail of our lives, maintaining further this selfish preoccupation so characteristic of the alcoholic.

The remainder of the steps are just as simple, effective and straightforward.

By over-emphasizing basic concepts such as resentment, selfishness, dishonesty, powerlessness, unmanageability or fear, we present a very difficult and often impossible to understand attempt at a psychological solution to alcoholism which was never the intention of our founders. These simple concepts require only acceptance, not endless analysis, to be effective in treating alcoholism.

Many if not most treatment centers that claim to be 12 step based create their own complicated and protracted methods, calling them "steps", requiring still sick alcoholics to write volumes analyzing these same simple concepts, further leading the confused alcoholic to more confusion.

These complicated methods of working and studying the steps have so diluted, altered, and in many ways stripped AA of the original spiritual principles that once made the steps so effective, that as of this writing it is estimated that there is only

21

a 5% to 7% recovery rate in AA

If you are an alcoholic (or addicted to other substances) you owe it to yourself and those you may attempt to help to take the steps in the manner in which they are intended to be taken. Of course we are all free at any time to work or study our way through the steps using more detailed and complicated methods.

Most everyone who has taken the steps as described in this book have found this to be a simple and effective way of achieving what AA was designed to do: connect with a higher power that could relieve our alcoholism. It is how knowledgeable sponsors or other early members of AA would take newcomers through the 12 Steps.

As aforementioned, in the early days of AA, many groups achieved a high (50% to 60%) recovery rate simply by guiding newcomers through the steps as they are presented in the book Alcoholics Anonymous, and then directing the newcomer to do the same.

"I have felt that AA is a group unto themselves and their best results can be had under their own guidance, as a result of their philosophy. Any therapeutic or philosophic procedure which can prove a recovery rate of 50% to 60% must merit our consideration." (Dr. Kirby Collier, psychiatrist, from The Medical View On AA appendix III Alcoholics Anonymous, 1944)

As AA members have disregarded the simple and proven program of recovery presented in The Big Book, or added their own interpretation or additions to the 12 Steps, the effectiveness of AA to actually help alcoholics has diminished to the point where statistically AA has almost no effect on relieving the suffering of alcoholism.

When I joined AA in 1981 there were an estimated two million members worldwide. Today, there is still an estimated two million members, meaning AA hasn't grown in over thirty years, yet when people followed the directions found in The

22

Big Book, the majority of people stayed sober and the growth of AA was exponential. (AA grew from zero members to two million members from 1939 to 1976, just 37 years.)

Since its inception, the spiritual nature of AA has been challenged from both inside and outside AA. Many in AA will cite various traditions (or parts of traditions) to justify the view that AA is anything that anyone says it is. The most overlooked and avoided tradition is Tradition 5, which states, "Each Alcoholics Anonymous group ought to be a **spiritual entity** having but one primary purpose - that of carrying its message (recovery through the 12 Steps) to the alcoholic who still suffers."

When AA was growing rapidly, and many individuals and groups were engaging in activities our founders felt may not allow for the effectiveness and future growth of AA, they decided on developing a set of traditions to guide the way that individuals and groups carry the message of recovery. Thinking that alcoholics will not tolerate being told what to do, they presented these guidelines, as they presented the steps, as "suggestions," hoping not to alienate any member or group.

The result of this lack of clear direction has been indifference by many AA members towards any of the "suggestions" regarding recovery and individual or group behavior.

Certainly many groups today are not spiritual entities and are not interested in carrying a spiritual message of recovery through the 12 Steps. This will likely not change unless individual members take responsibility for their own sobriety and the message they carry to others. Alcoholics as a rule abhor change and much prefer what they perceive as an easier, softer way.

The irony here is that the easier, softer way is found in following the program the way it is designed. There is great liberation and freedom from alcoholism, and self-centered behavior, in actually taking the 12 Steps and guiding others through the steps, as opposed to the grim and tenuous sobriety some experience by simply not drinking and going to meetings, or by using other methods of "step work" not described in The Big Book.

As AA increasingly disregarded the spiritual solution to allow for all points of view of what constitutes recovery in the AA 12 step program, (including not taking the 12 Steps at all), AA has lost its effectiveness almost completely, and fellow alcoholics suffer and die needlessly.

They suffer and die needlessly so that individuals can "work" their own individual program of recovery with no consideration of whether the resulting message we are presenting is of any real effectiveness to other alcoholics.

Have we as individual AA members taken the steps and "fit ourselves to be of service to God and those about us" (page 77, The Big Book), or have we simply found a way to avoid drinking, with no experience, strength, or hope to offer another alcoholic except "don't drink and go to meetings"?

Those that have stayed sober by gritting their teeth and simply not drinking and going to meetings, and those who selfishly say "if it's not broke, don't fix it", have greatly contributed to a now almost ineffective program which hasn't grown in over thirty years. It is time to face the fact that AA is broke, and only when responsible members actually fit themselves to carry the message of the spiritual solution, will AA return to an effective program based on spiritual principles.

Those that scoff at Alcoholics Anonymous today and say that it does not work are right. For most of the suffering alcoholics who come through our doors, it does not. How could it if the only suggested program of recovery is never offered to those still suffering? As sponsors and AA members many of us have gone from offering a proven program of recovery, to presenting a complicated and protracted exercise having very little resemblance to the highly effective spiritual solution to alcoholism AA was designed to be.

At many AA meetings, instead of describing the only program of recovery AA has to offer, we toss slogans at

24

newcomers and offer distracting and ineffective group therapy and behavior modification. At speaker or speaker/discussion meetings many speakers share their drunk-a-log and a passing reference that AA has helped them, thinking that this is sharing their experience, strength and hope.

AA meetings should be a place where we carry the message of our experience of recovery through the 12 Steps, our strength received from a higher power, and our hope to continue to grow along spiritual lines and to continue to be of service to others.

At AA meetings today, some members who have not had a drink in many years, sound just like someone new to AA, with all the problems, grievances, and character defects of the newcomer.

AA meetings are not where we describe in minute details the events of our day or our unhappiness and frustrations with the people in our lives. This is not what is meant by rigorous honesty. This is simply more alcoholic self-centeredness. No wonder very few alcoholics continue to come to meetings when this discouraging and inaccurate example of recovery is presented. No wonder that today very few alcoholics ever achieve comfortable, contented, useful sobriety.

Why do we have meetings?

"...It became customary to set apart one night a week for a meeting to be **attended by anyone or everyone interested in a spiritual way of life**. Aside from fellowship and sociability, the prime object was to provide a time and place where **new people might bring their problems**." (From Chapter 11, A Vision For You, The Big Book)

Notice that this quote from Bill Wilson says meetings are based on a spiritual way of life and "Where new people might bring their problems" related to this new spiritual way of life. AA meetings were never meant to be a place for general discussion of everyone's problems of the day or an airing of grievances, and certainly it was not the intention of our founders to hold meeting after meeting of group therapy.

The following is a definition of group therapy: "Group therapy is a form of psychosocial treatment where a small group of patients meet regularly to talk, interact, and discuss problems with each other and the group leader (therapist)." This is an apt description of many modern AA meetings with an un-qualified chairperson acting as therapist and participants seeking a human resolution to everyones problems.

AA is not designed to solve everyone's individual problems or to find a resolution for everyone's grievances. Our singleness of purpose should remind us that we unite around our common problem, alcoholism, and how we recover from alcoholism by utilizing spiritual principles.

The spiritual solution to alcoholism achieved through the teaching and practice of the 12 Steps does not require the absence of problems. Continued sobriety is not contingent on the possibility of drinking over our individual problems or grievances.

Hopefully, once we come to AA, a knowledgeable sponsor will have taken us through the steps as presented in the Big Book and instructed us to continue to take personal inventory, continue with daily prayer and meditation, and continue to help others, as Bill and Dr. Bob did.

It is with personal inventory that we examine the cause of our self-centered upsets, and in prayer and meditation we seek our higher power's help in relieving our self-centered views. By continually rehashing our problems, we simply reinforce them, and the more we do this, the more suffering we create for others and ourselves.

When Bill Wilson first achieved sobriety, he had significant physical, mental, financial and spiritual problems. There were no meetings for Bill to air his daily problems and resentments. How did he stay sober? Bill was finally able to achieve sobriety by utilizing the spiritual principles presented by his sponsor Ebby T., and then seeking out other alcoholics to help

THE SPIRITUAL SOLUTION TO ALCOHOLISM

recover.

Bill could not stay sober until he put his personal problems aside and began to help alcoholics by applying the spiritual principles found in the 12 Steps. He had to take action using the spiritual toolkit laid at his feet.

When a new person comes to an AA meeting with their troubles, we show them that despite what may be happening during the daily events of our lives, we stay sober by practicing the principles of the 12 Steps. This means that on a daily basis, we practice steps 10, 11 and 12. We take a personal inventory to find out our part in our upset and how and where we are acting in accordance with God's will and where we are not. We pray and meditate daily to improve our conscious contact with our higher power. We then acknowledge our spiritual awakening by living with integrity and presenting this same spiritual program to others in need of it.

"When we retire at night, we constructively review our day. Were we resentful, selfish, dishonest or afraid? Do we owe an apology? Have we kept something to ourselves which should be discussed with another person at once? Were we kind and loving toward all? What could we have done better? Were we thinking of ourselves most of the time? Or were we thinking of what we could do for others, of what we could pack into the stream of life? But we must be careful not to drift into worry, remorse or morbid reflection, for that would diminish our usefulness to others. After making our review we ask God's forgiveness and inquire what corrective measures should be taken." "On awakening let us think about the twenty-four hours ahead. We consider our plans for the day. Before we begin, we ask God to direct our thinking, especially asking that it be divorced from self-pity, dishonest or self-seeking motives. Under these conditions we can employ our mental faculties with assurance, for after all God gave us brains to use. Our thought-life will be placed on a much higher plane when our thinking is cleared of wrong

27

motives." (The Big Book page 86, paragraphs 1 and 2)

At meetings we talk about how we actually stay sober by practicing the steps and by explaining how the spiritual solution manifests in our lives. If we do not talk about our own recovery through the steps, how will newcomers understand what the "suggested" program of recovery actually entails? This is what is meant by "sharing our experience, strength, and hope."

AA members, and AA groups, should be ever mindful of how effective is the message being presented, and is the message consistent with what is presented in The Big Book?

Can we as a fellowship continue to justify the extremely low recovery rate found today in AA by excusing the failings of the program on newcomers or returning members who simply did not go to enough meetings or not "work" some complicated program full of mixed messages? Can we continue to offer nothing to the AA member with many years of sobriety who has not changed at all save for not drinking, and is still deeply troubled by the same character defects they came to AA with?

We certainly owe it to ourselves and to all others seeking recovery from alcoholism to offer the clear and simple program of recovery presented in our textbook. We are all responsible for the ineffectiveness of AA today.

A 5% to 7% recovery rate is almost no recovery at all.

The simple explanation as to why AA has lost its effectiveness is that as a fellowship we have relegated the spiritual nature of AA to a secondary or even unnecessary status. AA is a highly effective treatment for alcoholism when utilized as it was meant to be.

Unfortunately, due to influences both inside and outside of AA, many meetings and many groups are not even willing to discuss a higher power or point people towards the steps. Many people who consider themselves members of AA believe that they have no responsibility to present the only "suggested" program of recovery because it is only a suggestion.

There is no other program of recovery suggested in The Big Book. Nowhere in The Big Book will one find the notions of "90 meetings in 90 days", "don't drink and go to meetings", "meeting makers make it," or any of the other slogans. The hard truth is that most people who only make meetings do not make it. Members who have not had a drink in many years advise newcomers to avoid the steps and just "take the slogans." This is self-centered advice leading many back to drinking.

Those relying on slogans for their sobriety often advise newcomers that the spiritual nature of the program is optional and even unnecessary. Even those that believe the steps may be useful advise that newcomers should not even consider taking the steps for many months or even years. This is also the position of many treatment centers. The simple and straightforward steps as presented in The Big Book are designed so that the newcomer can take them immediately without becoming lost in confusing and protracted psychological exercise.

If the only suggested program of recovery is the 12 Steps as presented in the Big Book, what else will give people the best chance at comfortable, contented sobriety than actually taking the steps? AA is after all a 12 step program. Nothing else.

There certainly is a need for treatment centers as they provide a safe place for detoxification, rest, and hopefully an accurate introduction to AA. Unfortunately, many people leave the therapeutic setting of treatment centers believing that daily group therapy and behavior modification is also part of AA. Many treatment centers devise their own methods based on psychological theory, calling these complicated methods "steps" when in fact these steps bear little resemblance to the 12 Steps of Alcoholics Anonymous. This leads to even more confusion and discouragement and, for the most part, we as AA members do very little to minimize this confusion and offer encouragement with a clear explanation of the program of recovery.

Despite the first chapter in The Big Book, The Doctor's Opinion, which states that conventional psychology does not have any real effect on treating the alcoholic, and that alcoholics do respond to a spiritual solution, many meetings today are nothing more than un-moderated group therapy, amateur psychoanalysis, and a misguided attempt at behavior modification.

From The Doctor's Opinion:

"Many types do not respond to the ordinary psychological approach" and "...among physicians, the general opinion seems to be that most chronic alcoholics are doomed." Dr. Silkworth also tells us what does work: "Once a psychic change has occurred, the very same person who seemed doomed, who had so many problems he despaired ever solving them, suddenly finds himself able to control his desire for alcohol, the only effort necessary being that required to follow a few simple rules."

The psychic change Dr. Silkworth refers to is found in taking the 12 Steps. The few simple rules to follow are the simple directions to taking the 12 Steps found in The Big Book and used in The Spiritual Solution Workshop.

Treatment centers would likely achieve a much higher recovery rate by including, as part of alcoholism and addiction treatment, the 12 Steps as described in this book as early as possible during treatment. Alcoholics and addicts would then understand what the AA program of recovery is and be well on their way to helping other alcoholics achieve sobriety and so strengthen their own sobriety.

Bill Wilson, one of the co-founders of Alcoholics Anonymous, along with Dr. Bob Smith, stated in a Grapevine article (an AA monthly publication) in February of 1958:

"Sobriety, freedom from alcohol through the **teaching and practice of the 12 Steps** is the sole purpose of an AA group."

Go to many meetings today and try to discern any spiritual purpose, or presentation of the message of recovery through the taking and teaching of the 12 Steps.

It is not surprising to see why AA has failed to "show people precisely how we have recovered." As individual members, we have failed in carrying the simple program of recovery presented in The Big Book. We as AA members have the responsibility to first "fit ourselves to be of service to God and those about us" (page 77, The Big Book) by taking the 12 Steps as presented in the Big Book, and then take others through the 12 Steps.

This is how we progress from being restless, irritable and discontented, to having comfortable, contented sobriety and living healthy, useful lives in service to others. This is the program of recovery. This is how we recover.

Many AA members have devised other methods of "working", "studying", or "analyzing" the steps that are much more complicated and not nearly as effective as simply taking the steps in the straightforward way described in The Big Book. Even though these other methods differ significantly from what is presented in The Big Book, most will insist that these methods are the steps as presented in The Big Book.

Analyzing and studying of the spiritual solution was never the intention of the writers of the Big Book and is not the program of recovery presented in our textbook.

There is no hidden secret about the steps. None of us need a "step expert" to take the steps. We simply need someone who has taken the steps as presented in The Big Book and is willing to be our guide.

The 12 Steps as they are presented in the Big Book are to be taken systematically in order, in one sitting. If the reader doubts this, read Bills' Story in The Big Book.

31

Bill Wilson, still suffering from his last drunk, took the steps as they were then, simple spiritual principles taken from the Oxford group and a few other sources, with his sponsor Ebby T in one afternoon while sitting on his hospital bed. Bill then immediately began to find where he could do the same with other alcoholics. No one told him he was too sick to take the steps or that he did not have enough sober time to help other alcoholics. None of us would be here today if someone had discouraged Bill in the manner we discourage many newcomers today.

Bill's great breakthrough was his understanding that in order for him to stay sober, he must start helping other alcoholics immediately. It is in the teaching and practice of the 12 Steps that we strengthen our own recovery and deepen our own spiritual awakening. It is through service to others that we gain liberation from our extreme self-centeredness and become increasingly God-centered.

Experience has shown that the method described in this book and presented in The Big Book works just as well for groups taking the 12 Steps together in one-day workshops as it does for the sponsor taking their sponsee through the 12 Steps one-on-one.

As of this writing (February 2012), approximately 500 people in recovery have participated in The Spiritual Solution Workshops, and most of them have stayed clean and sober. Although no statistics are kept for obvious reasons, I am in contact with many of these folks, and I would estimate that 80% to 85% are maintaining their sobriety and being of effective service to other alcoholics.

The participants in these workshops have ranged in age from their teens to their eighties, and from those with a day or two of sobriety to some with 30 or more years of continuous sobriety.

Almost to a person, the responses after a workshop elicited joyful surprise at discovering how simple and effective the 12 step program of recovery is when the steps are taken as they are meant to be, and as described in the book Alcoholics Anonymous.

The spiritual solution program of recovery is simply this:
- Acknowledging our alcoholism
- A willingness to believe in a power greater than human power
- Deciding that a Higher Power would provide our recovery
- Identifying our self-centered character defects
- In prayer and meditation asking our Higher Power to remove these defects of character
- Deepening our relationship with a Higher Power once these blocks to the relationship are removed
- Helping other alcoholics do the same

This is what the steps are designed to do and what they achieve so effectively as long as they are followed as presented. Doing this is what keeps us sober.

To those who are not seeking a spiritual solution to their alcoholism, AA probably will not work, as its effectiveness is in the 12 Steps whose sole purpose is finding and establishing a relationship with a higher power that will relieve one's alcoholism.

As the reader will soon experience, there is no endless writing describing what each step means and how the steps may somehow be relevant to your life. There is no need to study or analyze the steps. The book "The Twelve Steps and Twelve Traditions" is not used. The Twelve Steps and Twelve Traditions is Bill Wilson's commentary on the steps and was never meant as instruction. Using Bill's commentary as instruction will only lead to more confusion. There is no test after step 12.

The only "test" is have you fit yourself to be of service to God and those about you by actually taking the steps. You will know that you have passed the test as you continue to grow along spiritual lines and you begin taking others through the steps from The Big Book.

As The Big Book describes and these guidelines point out, the steps are simply a few questions (Steps 1, 2, and 6), a few prayers (Steps 3, 7, and 11) a few statements of fact (steps 6, 8 and 12) and some positive actions and commitments (Steps 4, 5, 10, 11 and 12).

Once the steps are taken, in order to keep ourselves in fit spiritual condition and maintain our freedom from alcohol, we take a personal inventory, we develop a daily prayer and meditation practice, and we seek out other alcoholics to help by guiding them through the steps.

By adding layer upon layer of embellishments to a simple and straightforward method designed to give all alcoholics a chance of recovery, we have made the 12 Steps much more difficult, much less effective, and in many ways impossible for the newcomer.

If the reader is sponsoring people through taking the steps, please try the method presented here and described in our textbook.

If you want a spiritual solution to your alcoholism, find a sponsor who has actually taken the steps as presented in The Big Book and seek their guidance. It is your best chance at comfortable, contented, useful sobriety.

Please head the words of Herbert Spencer found in The Big Book at the end of the chapter Spiritual Experience (appendix 2) "There is a principle which is a bar against all information, which is proof against all arguments, and which cannot fail to keep a man in everlasting ignorance – that principle is contempt prior to investigation."

I wish you great success and permanent sobriety as you now actually take the steps.

Part 2
The Spiritual Solution Workshop

The Spiritual Solution Steps From The Big Book Workshop Introduction

Today we will take all twelve steps as they are presented in The Big Book, the textbook of Alcoholics Anonymous. The method we are using is very similar to the way our founders, Bill W. and Dr. Bob, and other early members of AA took other alcoholics through the steps, most while they were still in a hospital, a day or two sober, certainly very early in their recovery.

At that time, if you came to AA, you took the steps immediately, and a great majority of people stayed sober (not the small percentage that achieve sobriety today).

Notice the word 'took' - as opposed to worked, studied or analyzed. The steps are meant to be taken as presented in The Big Book.

The notion that in early sobriety we are too befuddled to take these steps belies the fact that we are seeking a spiritual solution to our drinking problem. We seek a *higher power* to provide our recovery. Our physical, mental, emotional or spiritual state has no bearing on when the spiritual solution will be effective. A higher power that can relieve our alcoholism can certainly transcend the physical effects of alcoholism.

The method of taking the 12 Steps is presented in The Big Book in a way that with the guidance of a qualified sponsor any newcomer can effectively take all 12 Steps immediately upon coming to AA. In fact, when an alcoholic first comes to AA is when the alcoholic is most receptive to taking the 12 Steps.

The following Big Book excerpt is from Bill's story and we can clearly see that Bill, while still detoxing in the hospital, is taken through the steps as they were then, by his sponsor Ebby T:

At the hospital I was separated from alcohol for the last time. Treatment seemed wise, for I showed signs of delirium tremens.

There I humbly offered myself to God, as I then understood Him, to do with me as He would. I placed myself unreservedly under His care and direction. I admitted for the first time that of myself I was nothing; that without Him I was lost. I ruthlessly faced my sins and became willing to have my new-found Friend take them away, root and branch. I have not had a drink since.

My schoolmate visited me, and I fully acquainted him with my problems and deficiencies. We made a list of people I had hurt or toward whom I felt resentment. I expressed my entire willingness to approach these individuals, admitting my wrong. Never was I to be critical of them. I was to right all such matters to the utmost of my ability.

I was to test my thinking by the new God-consciousness within. Common sense would thus become uncommon sense. I was to sit quietly when in doubt, asking only for direction and strength to meet my problems as He would have me. Never was I to pray for myself, except as my requests bore on my usefulness to others. Then only might I expect to receive. But that would be in great measure.

My friend promised when these things were done I would enter upon a new relationship with my Creator; that I would have the elements of a way of living which answered all my problems. Belief in the power of God, plus enough willingness, honesty and humility to establish and maintain the new order of things, were the essential requirements.

Simple, but not easy; a price had to be paid. It meant

destruction of self-centeredness. I must turn in all things to the Father of Light who presides over us all.

These were revolutionary and drastic proposals, but the moment I fully accepted them, the effect was electric. There was a sense of victory, followed by such a peace and serenity as I had never known. There was utter confidence. I felt lifted up, as though the great clean wind of a mountain top blew through and through. God comes to most men gradually, but His impact on me was sudden and profound.

For a moment I was alarmed, and called my friend, the doctor, to ask if I were still sane. He listened in wonder as I talked.

Finally he shook his head saying, "Something has happened to you I don't understand. But you had better hang on to it. Anything is better than the way you were." The good doctor now sees many men who have such experiences. He knows that they are real.

While I lay in the hospital the thought came that there were thousands of hopeless alcoholics who might be glad to have what had been so freely given me. Perhaps I could help some of them. They in turn might work with others.

My friend had emphasized the absolute necessity of demonstrating these principles in all my affairs. Particularly was it imperative to work with others as he had worked with me. Faith without works was dead, he said. And how appallingly true for the alcoholic! For if an alcoholic failed to perfect and enlarge his spiritual life through work and self-sacrifice for others, he could not survive the certain trials and low spots ahead. If he did not work, he would surely drink again, and if he drank, he would surely die. Then faith would be dead indeed. With us it is just like that.

In the early days of Alcoholics Anonymous there were no excuses or apologies made for the spiritual nature of this program. AA is after all a "spiritual solution to the drinking problem." We are in AA to find and connect to a higher power that can relieve our alcoholism. We learn that no human power can relieve our alcoholism.

Expecting fellowship alone to provide the recovery of the 12 Steps is relying on human power and is a grave mistake.

(Quotes from the Big Book are from the First Edition, page and paragraph as noted)

(17:3) The tremendous fact for every one of us is that we have discovered a common solution. We have a way out on which we can absolutely agree, and upon which we can join in brotherly and harmonious action. This is the great news this book carries to those who suffer from alcoholism.

(25:1) There is a solution. Almost none of us liked the self-searching, the leveling of our pride, the confession of shortcomings which the process requires for its successful consummation. But we saw that it really worked in others, and we had come to believe in the hopelessness and futility of life as we had been living it. When, therefore, we were approached by those in whom the problem had been solved, there was nothing left for us but to pick up the simple kit of spiritual tools laid at our feet. We have found much of heaven and we have been rocketed into a fourth dimension of existence of which we had not even dreamed.

(25:2) The great fact is just this, and nothing less: That we have had deep and effective spiritual experiences which have revolutionized our whole attitude toward life, toward our fellows and toward God's universe. The central fact of our lives today is the absolute certainty that our Creator has entered into our hearts and lives in a way which is indeed miraculous. He has commenced to accomplish those things for us which we could never do by ourselves.

(25:3) If you are as seriously alcoholic as we were, we

believe there is no middle-of-the-road solution. We were in a position where life was becoming impossible, and if we had passed into the region from which there is no return through human aid, we had but two alternatives: One was to go on to the bitter end, blotting out the consciousness of our intolerable situation as best we could; and the other, to accept spiritual help. This we did because we honestly wanted to, and were willing to make the effort.

(568:2) Most of us think this awareness of a Power greater than ourselves is the essence of spiritual experience. Our more religious members call it "God-consciousness." Most emphatically we wish to say that any alcoholic capable of honestly facing his problems in the light of our experience can recover, provided he does not close his mind to all spiritual concepts. He can only be defeated by an attitude of intolerance or belligerent denial. We find that no one need have difficulty with the spirituality of the program. Willingness, honesty and open mindedness are the essentials of recovery. But these are indispensable. "There is a principle which is a bar against all information, which is proof against all arguments and which cannot fail to keep a man in everlasting ignorance—that principle is contempt prior to investigation."

Taking the 12 Steps as presented in the Big Book is the spiritual solution to alcoholism.

Well meaning members that misinterpret the traditions, particularly tradition 3, "the only requirement for membership is a desire to stop drinking" as meaning that we do not have to do anything as members of AA except show up at meetings and "share" our problems, are simply wrong. Out of fear or a lack of understanding, we fail to present the only program of recovery offered in Alcoholics Anonymous. AA is a spiritual solution to the drinking problem and the spiritual solution requires that we take action in the form of a few simple steps.

The desire to stop drinking gets you a seat. Taking the steps keeps you in your seat.

Sayings such as make "90 meetings in 90 days", "meeting makers make it", "don't drink and go to meetings", "no relationships in the first year", "wait for the miracle" and many others that are said so often that many people believe that these sayings are a part of the program of recovery. They are not. Though they are good suggestions, none are a substitute for taking the 12 Steps. Slogans will never provide the comfortable, contented and useful sobriety that recovery achieved through the 12 Steps, in connection with a power greater than ourselves, can and will. Guaranteed. (See Step 12, The Big Book, page 89, paragraph 1)

In "How It Works", we are reminded of three pertinent ideas:

- **That we were alcoholic and could not manage our own lives**
- **That probably no human power could have relieved our alcoholism**
- **That God could and would, if he were sought.**

Relying on "fellowship" alone is relying on human power. Many people fail to achieve permanent, comfortable, contented sobriety because they rely on human power alone. It does not work. Relying on the group, our sponsor, our "network," or our therapist to keep us sober is relying on human power.

The fellowship and general AA meetings are not where we gain sobriety. AA meetings are where we share our recovery through the twelve steps, our understanding of the spiritual solution, and where we can be of service to others with our disease.

The AA program of recovery is not a psychological solution to the drinking problem, despite what often seems like group therapy at meetings. If this appears to be at odds with what many groups and meetings are focused on, it is. If group therapy were effective in helping alcoholics recover, then Dr. Silkworth would not have written what he wrote in "The Doctors Opinion." (Reviewed in step 1)

AA and specifically the 12 Steps as presented in The Big Book is the SPIRITUAL SOLUTION to the drinking problem. The 12 Steps lead to a spiritual awakening, as stated in step 12.

We are not so concerned with our problems of the day as we are our spiritual condition. As stated in The Big Book, it is not our problems that made us drink, it is our behavior, specifically self-centered behavior.

Many of us are led to believe by the structure of AA today, that we must focus on our problems, talk to our sponsors every day with our problem *du-jour*, connect with our network, and then we are often advised to bring our problems to a meeting. What can be more self-centered than a constant preoccupation with our problems? As stated on page 77 of The Big Book: "The purpose of sobriety is to fit ourselves to be of maximum service to God and those about us." How is this selfish focusing on our problems going to help us or others? How is this being of service to God and those about us?

We take the 12 Steps to be relieved of the bondage of self, including self-centered focus on individual problems.

The steps do require that we take action. It is implied by the use of the word "steps". If you want the benefits that walking exercise will give you, you will not get those benefits by reading about the experience of walking. If you want the benefits of the steps, reading Bills commentary in the 12 and 12 or just reading or "studying" the Big Book is just that, reading about the experience of taking the steps.

If you want comfortable, contented, lasting sobriety, you have to actually take the steps!

As alcoholics who have been blessed by the miracle of recovery, or soon will be, it is our responsibility to fit ourselves to carry this program of recovery to other alcoholics. This is precisely how we stay sober.

On page 77 it states, "the PURPOSE of sobriety is to FIT ourselves to be of service to God and those about us." The 12 Steps are how we FIT ourselves to be of service to God and those about us, to recover from alcoholism, and to help others recover from alcoholism.

Neither Bill nor Bob could stay sober UNTIL they took the steps as they were then, spiritual principles taken from the Oxford Group and a few other sources, and then helped other alcoholics achieve sobriety. They had to fit themselves BEFORE they could effectively share what they learned of staying sober with others like themselves.

During this workshop we will read the steps as presented in the Big Book. We have selected references to each step from the Big Book for the purpose of this workshop and for clarity. Once we have read the steps, we will take the steps.

Workshop handouts

(Steps 4 and 5 Instructions, Step 4 Definitions and 4th Step Inventory Checklists)

are available for free download at www.johnh12steps.com.

Step 1

We admitted we were powerless over alcohol, that our lives had become unmanageable

THE DOCTOR'S OPINION
(From the book Alcoholics Anonymous)

WE, OF Alcoholics Anonymous, are more than one hundred men and women who have recovered from a seemingly hopeless state of mind and body. To show other alcoholics precisely how we have recovered is the main purpose of this book. For them, we hope these pages will prove so convincing that no further authentication will be necessary. We think this account of our experiences will help everyone to better understand the alcoholic. Many do not comprehend that the alcoholic is a very sick person. And besides, we are sure that our way of living has its advantages for all.

To Whom It May Concern:

I have specialized in the treatment of alcoholism for many years.

In late 1934 I attended a patient who, though he had been a competent businessman of good earning capacity, was an alcoholic of a type I had come to regard as hopeless.

In the course of his third treatment he acquired certain ideas concerning a possible means of recovery. As part of his rehabilitation he commenced to present his conceptions to other alcoholics, impressing upon them that they must do likewise with still others. This has become the basis of a rapidly growing fellowship of these men and their families. This man and over one hundred others appear to have recovered.

I personally know scores of cases who were of the type with whom **other methods had failed completely.**

These facts appear to be of extreme medical importance; because of the extraordinary possibilities of rapid growth inherent in this group they may mark a new epoch in the annals of alcoholism. These men may well have a remedy for thousands of such situations.

You may rely absolutely on anything they say about themselves.

Very truly yours,
William D. Silkworth, M.D.

The physician who, at our request, gave us this letter, has been kind enough to enlarge upon his views in another statement which follows. In this statement he confirms what we who have suffered alcoholic torture must believe —that the body of the alcoholic is quite as abnormal as his mind. It did not satisfy us to be told that we could not control our drinking just because we were maladjusted to life, that we were in full flight from reality, or were outright mental defectives. These things were true to some extent, in fact, to a considerable extent with some of us. But we are sure that our bodies were sickened as well. In our belief, any picture of the alcoholic which leaves out this physical factor is incomplete.

The doctor's theory that we have an allergy to alcohol interests us. As laymen, our opinion as to its soundness may, of course, mean little. But as ex-problem drinkers, we can say that his explanation makes good sense. It explains many things for which we cannot otherwise account.

The doctor writes:

We doctors have realized for a long time that some form of moral psychology was of urgent importance to alcoholics, but its application presented difficulties beyond our conception. What with our ultra-modern standards, our scientific approach to everything, we are perhaps not well equipped to apply the powers of good that lie outside our synthetic knowledge.

Many years ago one of the leading contributors to this book came under our care in this hospital and while here he acquired some ideas which he put into practical application at once.

Later, he requested the privilege of being allowed to tell his story to other patients here and with some misgiving, we consented. The cases we have followed through have been most interesting; in fact, many of them are amazing. The unselfishness of these men as we have come to know them, the entire absence of profit motive, and their community spirit, is indeed inspiring to one who has labored long and wearily in this alcoholic field. They believe in themselves, and still more in the Power which pulls chronic alcoholics back from the gates of death.

Of course an alcoholic ought to be freed from his physical craving for liquor, and this often requires a definite hospital procedure, before psychological measures can be of maximum benefit. We believe, and so suggested a few years ago, that the action of alcohol on these chronic alcoholics is a manifestation of an allergy; that the phenomenon of craving is limited to this class and never occurs in the average temperate drinker. These allergic types can never safely use alcohol in any form at all; and once having formed the habit and found they cannot break it, once having lost their self-confidence, their reliance upon things human, their problems pile up on them and become astonishingly difficult to solve.

Frothy emotional appeal seldom suffices. The message

which can interest and hold these alcoholic people must have depth and weight. In nearly all cases, their ideals must be grounded in a power greater than themselves, if they are to re-create their lives.

Men and women drink essentially because they like the effect produced by alcohol. The sensation is so elusive that, while they admit it is injurious, they cannot after a time differentiate the true from the false. To them, their alcoholic life seems the only normal one. They are restless, irritable and discontented, unless they can again experience the sense of ease and comfort which comes at once by taking a few drinks—drinks which they see others taking with impunity. After they have succumbed to the desire again, as so many do, and the phenomenon of craving develops, they pass through the well-known stages of a spree, emerging remorseful, with a firm resolution not to drink again. This is repeated over and over, and unless this person can experience an entire psychic change there is very little hope of his recovery.

On the other hand—and strange as this may seem to those who do not understand—**once a psychic change has occurred, the very same person who seemed doomed, who had so many problems he despaired of ever solving them, suddenly finds himself easily able to control his desire for alcohol, the only effort necessary being that required to follow a few simple rules.**

Men have cried out to me in sincere and despairing appeal: "Doctor, I cannot go on like this! I have everything to live for! I must stop, but I cannot! You must help me!" Faced with this problem, if a doctor is honest with himself, he must sometimes feel his own inadequacy. Although he gives all that is in him, it often is not enough. One feels that something more than human power is needed to produce the essential psychic change. Though the aggregate of recoveries resulting from psychiatric effort is considerable, we physicians must admit we have made little impression upon the problem as a whole. Many types do not respond to the ordinary psychological approach.

I do not hold with those who believe that alcoholism is entirely a problem of mental control. I have had many men who had, for example, worked a period of months on some problem or business deal which was to be settled on a certain date, favorably to them. They took a drink a day or so prior to the date, and then the phenomenon of craving at once became paramount to all other interests so that the important appointment was not met. These men were not drinking to escape; they were drinking to overcome a craving beyond their mental control.

There are many situations which arise out of the phenomenon of craving which cause men to make the supreme sacrifice rather than continue to fight. The classification of alcoholics seems most difficult, and in much detail is outside the scope of this book. There are, of course, the psychopaths who are emotionally unstable. We are all familiar with this type. They are always "going on the wagon for keeps." They are over-remorseful and make many resolutions, but never a decision.

There is the type of man who is unwilling to admit that he cannot take a drink. He plans various ways of drinking. He changes his brand or his environment. There is the type who always believes that after being entirely free from alcohol for a period of time he can take a drink without danger. There is the manic-depressive type, who is, perhaps, the least understood by his friends, and about whom a whole chapter could be written.

Then there are types entirely normal in every respect except in the effect alcohol has upon them. They are often able, intelligent, friendly people. All these, and many others, have one symptom in common: they cannot start drinking without developing the phenomenon of craving. This phenomenon, as we have suggested, may be the manifestation of an allergy which differentiates these people, and sets them apart as a distinct entity. It has never been, by any treatment with which we are familiar, permanently eradicated. The only relief we have to suggest is entire abstinence.

This immediately precipitates us into a seething cauldron of debate. Much has been written pro and con, but among physicians, the general opinion seems to be that most chronic alcoholics are doomed.

What is the solution? Perhaps I can best answer this by relating one of my experiences.

About one year prior to this experience a man was brought in to be treated for chronic alcoholism. He had but partially recovered from a gastric hemorrhage and seemed to be a case of pathological mental deterioration. He had lost everything worthwhile in life and was only living, one might say, to drink. He frankly admitted and believed that for him there was no hope. Following the elimination of alcohol, there was found to be no permanent brain injury. He accepted the plan outlined in this book. One year later he called to see me, and I experienced a very strange sensation. I knew the man by name, and partly recognized his features, but there all resemblance ended. From a trembling, despairing, nervous wreck, had emerged a man brimming over with self-reliance and contentment. I talked with him for some time, but was not able to bring myself to feel that I had known him before. To me he was a stranger, and so he left me. A long time has passed with no return to alcohol.

When I need a mental uplift, I often think of another case brought in by a physician prominent in New York. The patient had made his own diagnosis, and deciding his situation hopeless, had hidden in a deserted barn determined to die. He was rescued by a searching party, and, in desperate condition, brought to me. Following his physical rehabilitation, he had a talk with me in which he frankly stated he thought the treatment a waste of effort, unless I could assure him, which no one ever had, that in the future he would have the "will power" to resist the impulse to drink.

His alcoholic problem was so complex, and his depression so great, that we felt his only hope would be through what we then called "moral psychology," and we doubted if even that would have any effect. However, he did become "sold" on the ideas contained in this book. He has not had a drink for a great many years. I see him now and then and he is as fine a specimen of manhood as one could wish to meet.

I earnestly advise every alcoholic to read this book through, and though perhaps he came to scoff, he may remain to pray.

William D. Silkworth, M.D.

Page and paragraph from the first edition of Alcoholics Anonymous in parentheses.

(30:1) Most of us have been unwilling to admit we were real alcoholics. No person likes to think he is bodily and mentally different from his fellows. Therefore, it is not surprising that our drinking careers have been characterized by countless vain attempts to prove we could drink like other people. The idea that somehow, someday he will control and enjoy his drinking is the great obsession of every abnormal drinker. The persistence of this illusion is astonishing. Many pursue it into the gates of insanity or death.

(30:2) **We learned that we had to fully concede to our innermost selves that we were alcoholics. This is the first step in recovery**. The delusion that we are like other people, or presently may be, has to be smashed.

(30:3) We alcoholics are men and women who have lost the ability to control our drinking. We know that no real alcoholic ever recovers control. All of us felt at times that we were regaining control, but such intervals - usually brief - were inevitably followed by still less control, which led in time to pitiful and incomprehensible demoralization. We are convinced to a man that alcoholics of our type are in the grip of a progressive illness. Over any considerable period we get worse, never better.

(30:4) We are like men who have lost their legs; they never grow new ones. Neither does there appear to be any kind of treatment which will make alcoholics of our kind like other men. We have tried every imaginable remedy. In some instances there has been brief recovery, followed always by a still worse relapse. Physicians who are familiar with alcoholism agree there is no such thing as making a normal drinker out of an alcoholic. Science may one day accomplish this, but it hasn't done so yet.

(34:2) For those who are unable to drink moderately the question is how to stop altogether. We are assuming, of course, that the reader desires to stop. Whether such a person can quit upon a nonspiritual basis depends upon the extent to which he has already lost the power to choose whether he will drink or not. Many of us felt that we had plenty of character. There was a tremendous urge to cease forever. Yet we found it impossible. This is the baffling feature of alcoholism as we know it - this utter inability to leave it alone, no matter how great the necessity or the wish.

~ ~ ~

Taking Step 1: (the group stands and individually answers)

Do you concede to your innermost self that you are an alcoholic?

If you can answer yes, you have taken Step 1.

~ ~ ~

Step 2

Came to believe that a power greater than ourselves could restore us to sanity

(8:1) (From Bills Story) No words can tell of the loneliness and despair I found in that bitter morass of self-pity. Quicksand stretched around me in all directions. I had met my match. I had been overwhelmed. Alcohol was my master.

(8:2) Trembling, I stepped from the hospital a broken man. Fear sobered me for a bit. Then came the insidious insanity of that first drink, and on Armistice Day 1934, I was off again. Everyone became resigned to the certainty that I would have to be shut up somewhere, or would stumble along to a miserable end. How dark it is before the dawn! In reality that was the beginning of my last debauch. I was soon to be catapulted into what I like to call the fourth dimension of existence. I was to know happiness, peace, and usefulness, in a way of life that is incredibly more wonderful as time passes.

(8:3) Near the end of that bleak November, I sat drinking in my kitchen. With a certain satisfaction I reflected there was enough gin concealed about the house to carry me through that night and the next day. My wife was at work. I wondered whether I dared hide a full bottle of gin near the head of our bed. I would need it before daylight.

(8:4) My musing was interrupted by the telephone. The cheery voice of an old school friend asked if he might come over. He was sober. It was years since I could remember his coming to New York in that condition. I was amazed. Rumor had it that he had been committed for alcoholic insanity. I wondered how he had escaped. Of course he would have dinner, and then I could drink openly with him. Unmindful of his welfare, I thought only of recapturing the spirit of other days. There was that time we had chartered an airplane to complete a jag! His coming was an oasis in this dreary desert of futility. The very thing - an oasis! Drinkers are like that.

(9:1) The door opened and he stood there, fresh-skinned and glowing. There was something about his eyes. He was inexplicably different. What had happened?

(9:2) I pushed a drink across the table. He refused it. Disappointed but curious, I wondered what had got into the fellow. He wasn't himself.

(9:3) "Come, what's this all about?" I queried.

(9:4) He looked straight at me. Simply, but smilingly, he said, "I've got religion."

(9:5) I was aghast. So that was it - last summer an alcoholic crackpot; now, I suspected, a little cracked about religion. He had that starry-eyed look. Yes, the old boy was on fire all right. But bless his heart, let him rant! Besides, my gin would last longer than his preaching.

(9:6) But he did no ranting. In a matter of fact way he told how two men had appeared in court, persuading the judge to suspend his commitment. They had told of a simple religious idea and a practical program of action. That was two months ago and the result was self-evident. It worked!

(9:7) He had come to pass his experience along to me - if I cared to have it. I was shocked, but interested. Certainly I was interested. I had to be, for I was hopeless.

(10:1) He talked for hours. Childhood memories rose before me. I could almost hear the sound of the preacher's voice as I sat, on still Sundays, way over there on the hillside; there was that proffered temperance pledge I

54

never signed; my grandfather's good natured contempt of some church folk and their doings; his insistence that the spheres really had their music; but his denial of the preacher's right to tell him how he must listen; his fearlessness as he spoke of these things just before he died; these recollections welled up from the past. They made me swallow hard.

(10:2) That war-time day in old Winchester Cathedral came back again.

(10:3) I had always believed in a Power greater than myself. I had often pondered these things. I was not an atheist. Few people really are, for that means blind faith in the strange proposition that this universe originated in a cipher and aimlessly rushes nowhere. My intellectual heroes, the chemists, the astronomers, even the evolutionists, suggested vast laws and forces at work. Despite contrary indications, I had little doubt that a mighty purpose and rhythm underlay all. How could there be so much of precise and immutable law, and no intelligence? I simply had to believe in a Spirit of the Universe, who knew neither time nor limitation. But that was as far as I had gone.

(10:4) With ministers, and the world's religions, I parted right there. When they talked of a God personal to me, who was love, superhuman strength and direction, I became irritated and my mind snapped shut against such a theory.

(11:1) To Christ I conceded the certainty of a great man, not too closely followed by those who claimed Him. His moral teaching - most excellent. For myself, I had adopted those parts which seemed convenient and not too difficult; the rest I disregarded.

(11:2) The wars which had been fought, the burnings and chicanery that religious dispute had facilitated, made me sick. I honestly doubted whether, on balance, the religions of mankind had done any good. Judging from what I had seen in Europe and since, the power of God in human affairs was negligible, the Brotherhood of Man a grim jest. If there was a Devil, he seemed the Boss Universal, and he certainly had me.

(11:3) But my friend sat before me, and he made the point-blank declaration that God had done for him what he could not do for himself. His human will had failed. Doctors had pronounced him incurable. Society was about to lock him up. Like myself, he had admitted complete defeat. Then he had, in effect, been raised from the dead, suddenly taken from the scrap heap to a level of life better than the best he had ever known!

(11:4) Had this power originated in him? Obviously it had not. There had been no more power in him than there was in me at the minute; and this was none at all.

(11:5) That floored me. It began to look as though religious people were right after all. Here was something at work in a human heart which had done the impossible. My ideas about miracles were drastically revised right then. Never mind the musty past; here sat a miracle directly across the kitchen table. He shouted great tidings.

(11:6) I saw that my friend was much more than inwardly reorganized. He was on a different footing. His roots grasped a new soil.

(12:1) Despite the living example of my friend there remained in me the vestiges of my old prejudice. The word God still aroused a certain antipathy. When the thought was expressed that there might be a God personal to me this feeling was intensified. I didn't like the idea. I could go for such conceptions as Creative Intelligence, Universal Mind or Spirit of Nature but I resisted the thought of a Czar of the Heavens, however loving His sway might be. I have since talked with scores of men who felt the same way.

(12:2) My friend suggested what then seemed a novel idea. He said, "Why don't you choose your own conception of God?"

(12:3) That statement hit me hard. It melted the icy intellectual mountain in whose shadow I had lived and shivered many years. I stood in the sunlight at last.

(12:4) **It was only a matter of being willing to believe in a Power greater than myself. Nothing more was required of me to make my beginning.** I saw that growth could start from that point. Upon a foundation of complete willingness I might build what I saw in my friend. Would I have it? Of course I would!

(12:5) Thus was I convinced that God is concerned with us humans when we want Him enough. At long last I saw, I felt, I believed. Scales of pride and prejudice fell from my eyes. A new world came into view.

(12:6) The real significance of my experience in the Cathedral burst upon me. For a brief moment, I had needed and wanted God. There had been a humble willingness to have Him with me - and He came. But soon the sense of His presence had been blotted out by worldly clamors, mostly those within myself. And so it had been ever since. How blind I had been.

(46:1) Yes, we of agnostic temperament have had these thoughts and experiences. Let us make haste to reassure you. We found that as soon as we were able to lay aside prejudice and express even a willingness to believe in a Power greater than ourselves, we commenced to get results, even though it was impossible for any of us to fully define or comprehend that Power, which is God.

(46:2) Much to our relief, we discovered we did not need to consider another's conception of God. Our own conception, however inadequate, was sufficient to make the approach and to effect a contact with Him. As soon as we admitted the possible existence of a Creative Intelligence, a Spirit of the Universe underlying the totality of things, we began to be possessed of a new sense of power and direction, provided we took other simple steps. We found that God does not make too hard terms with those who seek Him. To us, the Realm of Spirit is broad, roomy, all inclusive; never exclusive or forbidding to those who earnestly seek. It is open, we believe, to all men.

(47:1) When, therefore, we speak to you of God, we mean your own conception of God. This applies, too, to other spiritual expressions which you find in this book. Do not let any prejudice you may have against spiritual terms deter you from honestly asking yourself what they mean to you. At the start, this was all we needed to commence spiritual growth, to effect our first conscious relation with God as we understood Him. Afterward, we found ourselves accepting many things which then seemed entirely out of reach. That was growth, but if we wished to grow we had to begin somewhere. So we used our own conception, however limited it was.

(47:2) We needed to ask ourselves but one short question. **"Do I now believe, or am I even willing to believe, that there is a Power greater than myself?"** As soon as a man can say that he does believe, or is willing to believe, we emphatically assure him that he is on his way. It has been repeatedly proven among us that upon this simple cornerstone a wonderfully effective spiritual structure can be built.

Step 2 only asks of us to believe or to be willing to believe in a power greater than ourselves. This is a higher power of our own understanding. Developing and deepening our understanding of a Higher Power is what the remaining steps will accomplish. Remember that we are seeking a spiritual solution, not a religious solution.

The simple recognition that we are a group of once-hopeless alcoholics who are now sober is, for many, a demonstration of a power "greater than ourselves."

If you do not now believe in a power greater than your self, are you willing to change your mind? This is all Step 2 asks of us.

~ ~ ~

Taking Step 2: (the group stands and individually answers)

Do you now believe, or are you even willing to believe in a power greater than yourself?

If you can answer yes, you have taken Step 2.

~ ~ ~

Step 3

Made a decision to turn our will and our lives over to the care of God as we understood God

(13:1) At the hospital I was separated from alcohol for the last time. Treatment seemed wise, for I showed signs of delirium tremens.

(13:2) There I humbly offered myself to God, as I then understood Him, to do with me as He would. I placed myself unreservedly under His care and direction. I admitted for the first time that of myself I was nothing; that without Him I was lost. I ruthlessly faced my sins and became willing to have my new-found Friend take them away, root and branch. I have not had a drink since.

(44:4) If a mere code of morals or a better philosophy of life were sufficient to overcome alcoholism, many of us would have recovered long ago. But we found that such codes and philosophies did not save us, no matter how much we tried. We could wish to be moral, we could wish to be philosophically comforted, in fact, we could will these things with all our might, but the needed power wasn't there. Our human resources, as marshaled by the will, were not sufficient; they failed utterly.

(53:2) When we became alcoholics, crushed by a self-imposed crisis we could not postpone or evade, we had to fearlessly face the proposition that either God is everything or else He is nothing. God either is, or He isn't.

What was our choice to be?

(53:3) Arrived at this point, we were squarely confronted with the question of faith. We couldn't duck the issue. Some of us had already walked far over the Bridge of Reason toward the desired shore of faith. The outlines and the promise of the New Land had brought luster to tired eyes and fresh courage to flagging spirits. Friendly hands had stretched out in welcome. We were grateful that Reason had brought us so far. But somehow, we couldn't quite step ashore. Perhaps we had been leaning too heavily on Reason that last mile and we did not like to lose our support.

(53:4) That was natural, but let us think a little more closely. Without knowing it, had we not been brought to where we stood by a certain kind of faith? For did we not believe in our own reasoning? Did we not have confidence in our ability to think? What was that but a sort of faith? Yes, we had been faithful, abjectly faithful to the God of Reason. So, in one way or another, we discovered that faith had been involved all the time!

(55:5) In this book you will read the experience of a man who thought he was an atheist. His story is so interesting that some of it should be told now. His change of heart was dramatic, convincing, and moving.

(56:2) One night, when confined in a hospital, he was approached by an alcoholic who had known a spiritual experience. Our friend's gorge rose as he bitterly cried out: "If there is a God, He certainly hasn't done anything for me!" But later, alone in his room, he asked himself this question: "Is it possible that all the religious people I have known are wrong?" While pondering the answer he felt as though he lived in hell. Then, like a thunderbolt, a great thought came. It crowded out all else:

(56:3) "Who are you to say there is no God?"

(56:4) This man recounts that he tumbled out of bed to his knees. In a few seconds he was overwhelmed by a

62

conviction of the Presence of God. It poured over and through him with the certainty and majesty of a great tide at flood. The barriers he had built through the years were swept away. He stood in the Presence of Infinite Power and Love. He had stepped from bridge to shore. For the first time, he lived in conscious companionship with his Creator.

(56:5) Thus was our friend's cornerstone fixed in place. No later vicissitude has shaken it. His alcoholic problem was taken away. That very night, years ago, it disappeared.

(57:0) Save for a few brief moments of temptation the thought of drink has never returned; and at such times a great revulsion has risen up in him. Seemingly he could not drink even if he would. God had restored his sanity.

(57:1) What is this but a miracle of healing? Yet its elements are simple. Circumstances made him willing to believe. He humbly offered himself to his Maker - then he knew.

(57:2) Even so has God restored us all to our right minds. To this man, the revelation was sudden. Some of us grow into it more slowly. But He has come to all who have honestly sought Him.

(57:3) When we drew near to Him He disclosed Himself to us!

(60:3) Being convinced, we were at Step Three, which is that we decided to turn our will and our life over to God as we understood Him. Just what do we mean by that, and just what do we do?

(60:4) The first requirement is that we be convinced that any life run on self-will can hardly be a success. On that basis we are almost always in collision with something or somebody, even though our motives are good. Most people try to live by self-propulsion. Each person is like an actor who wants to run the whole show; is forever trying to arrange the lights, the ballet, the scenery and the rest of the players in his own way. If his arrangements would only stay put, if only people would do as he wished, the show would be great. Everybody, including himself, would be pleased. Life would be wonderful. In trying to make these arrangements our actor may sometimes be quite virtuous. He may be kind, considerate, patient, generous; even modest and self-sacrificing. On the other hand, he may be mean, egotistical, selfish and dishonest. But, as with most humans, he is more likely to have varied traits.

(61:1) What usually happens? The show doesn't come off very well. He begins to think life doesn't treat him right. He decides to exert himself more. He becomes, on the next occasion, still more demanding or gracious, as the case may be. Still the play does not suit him. Admitting he may be somewhat at fault, he is sure that other people are more to blame. He becomes angry, indignant, self-pitying. What is his basic trouble? Is he not really a self-seeker even when trying to be kind? Is he not a victim of the delusion that he can wrest satisfaction and happiness out of this world if he only manages well? Is it not evident to all the rest of the players that these are the things he wants? And do not his actions make each of them wish to retaliate, snatching all they can get out of the show? Is he not, even in his best moments, a producer of confusion rather than harmony?

(61:2) Our actor is self-centered - ego-centric, as people like to call it nowadays. He is like the retired business man who lolls in the Florida sunshine in the winter complaining of the sad state of the nation; the minister who sighs over the sins of the twentieth century; politicians and reformers who are sure all would be utopia if the rest of the world would only behave; the outlaw safe cracker who thinks society has wronged him; and the alcoholic who has lost all and is locked up. Whatever our protestations, are not most of us concerned with ourselves, our resentments, or our self-pity?

(62:1) Selfishness - self-centeredness! That, we think, is the root of our troubles. Driven by a hundred forms of fear, self-delusion, self-seeking, and self-pity, we step on the toes of our fellows and they retaliate. Sometimes they hurt us, seemingly without provocation, but we invariably find that at some time in the past we have made decisions based on self which later placed us in a position to be hurt.

(62:2) So our troubles, we think, are basically of our own making. They arise out of ourselves, and the alcoholic is an extreme example of self-will run riot, though he usually doesn't think so. Above everything, we alcoholics must be rid of this selfishness. We must, or it kills us! God makes that possible. And there often seems no way of entirely getting rid of self without His aid. Many of us had moral and philosophical convictions galore, but we could not live up to them even though we would have liked to. Neither could we reduce our self-centeredness much by wishing or trying on our own power. We had to have God's help.

(62:3) This is the how and why of it. First of all, we had to quit playing God. It didn't work. Next, we decided that hereafter in this drama of life, God was going to be our Director. He is the Principal; we are His agents. He is the Father, and we are His children. Most good ideas are simple, and this concept was the keystone of the new and triumphant arch through which we passed to freedom.

(63:1) When we sincerely took such a position, all sorts of remarkable things followed. We had a new Employer. Being all powerful, He provided what we needed, if we kept close to Him and performed His work well. Established on such a footing we became less and less interested in ourselves, our little plans and designs. More and more we became interested in seeing what we could contribute to life. As we felt new power flow in, as we enjoyed peace of mind, as we discovered we could face life successfully, as we became conscious of His presence, we began to lose our fear of today, tomorrow or the hereafter. We were reborn.

(63:2) We were now at Step Three. Many of us said to our Maker, as we understood Him: **"God, I offer myself to Thee**-to build with me and to do with me as Thou wilt. Relieve me of the bondage of self, that I may better do Thy will. Take away my difficulties, that victory over them may bear witness to those I would help of Thy Power, Thy Love, and Thy Way of life. May I do Thy will always!"

Now that we are willing to believe in a higher or greater power of our own understanding, we make a simple and strightforward decision to be guided by a higher power. The third step is simply a sincere prayer acknowledging that we are willing to have a higher power guide our recovery and our lives.

Please remember that our understanding of a higher power will develop and deepen as we take the remaining steps.

~ ~ ~

Taking Step 3: (Group recites prayer)

God, I offer myself to Thee-to build with me and to do with me as Thou wilt. Relieve me of the bondage of self, that I may better do Thy will. Take away my difficulties, that victory over them may bear witness to those I would help of Thy Power, Thy Love, and Thy Way of life. May I do Thy will always.

When you have sincerely said this prayer, you have taken Step 3.

~ ~ ~

Steps 4 and 5 Introduction

Many AA members have great confusion and fear about step 4 due to a misunderstanding of what this step is meant to accomplish, and how to exactly take step 4. By not following the clear directions in The Big Book, Step 4 has become a protracted and very confusing attempt at a written psycho-social analysis of a members entire life.

Step 5, once a simple converstation of the AA member's self-centered character defects and the harms caused by these defects, is now a lengthy confession and extended analysis of every negative event of the confused alcoholics life.

Steps 4 and 5 are not meant generate a major cathartic event facilitated by a sponsor. This would clearly be relying on human power. The step 4 inventory list and the step 5 review of the list with a sponsor or sharing partner is solely to identify the self-centered character defects listed in The Big Book on pages 64 to 70. Once identified these character defects can be relieved by a higher power through taking and practicing the remainder of the steps.

Most of the methods used today to "work" step 4 make this simple step much more complicated than ever intended. This has led a great number of alcoholics to become bogged down in extraneous details and never gain the insight necessary for an effective step 4.

The 12 Steps are intended to provide the spiritual solution to alcoholism. The step 4 inventory as presented in The Big Book is simply a detailed list of self-centered character defects. It is these character defects that block alcoholics from the spiritual solution and connecting to a higher power that will relieve their alcoholism.

As stated in The Big Book on page 62, first paragraph: "Selfishness – self-centeredness! That we think is the root of our troubles" as far as alcoholism is concerned. In the next paragraph The Big Book Authors write: "above EVERYTHING we alcoholics must be rid of this selfishness."

Step 4 is not intended to be an examination or analysis of deep-seated trauma or the effects of long suppressed misdeeds. On page 64, paragraph 2: "We searched out the flaws in our make-up." Examination or analysis of deep-seated emotional or psychological problems is beyond the intention and scope of a step 4 inventory and beyond the intention and scope of the 12 Steps.

Hopefully, a qualified sponsor or sharing partner will recognize this and if needed direct the sponsee to someone who is qualified to assist with these issues. Step 4 is very effective in identifying what self-centered character defects are an underlying part of any of these issues, which is precisely what step 4 is designed to do. It is not intended to be a psychological exercise or therapy of any kind. Becoming sidetracked into other issues will reduce or negate the effectiveness of step 4.

Sponsors should be clear that an inventory is not an in-depth detailed analysis of every incident of antisocial behavior. This results in complicating a simple process and will often prevent sponsees from a direct and effective way of relieving their alcoholism.

For example, for the purposes of a fourth step, it is not necessary to describe in detail physical or sexual abuse if the sponsee is reluctant. Simply using the words "abuse" or "traumatic event" is enough to then identify the underlying self-centered character defect. If harm has been done to the individual, fear may be an overriding emotion, and as fear is identified in the inventory, the individual will know that faith and love will aid in relieving the fear. If a long held resentment is present, it is instantly apparent that forgiveness is called for, with the help of a higher power.

Remember, we are not looking for justice for harms done to

68

us or for justification for our own actions.

If the person taking step 4 has stolen property, they may be reluctant for many reasons to initially admit to something that may cause further legal issues. Of primary importance is to examine the self-centered flaws in one's character in order to achieve permanent sobriety, in this case selfishness and dishonesty.

More involved issues can and should be dealt with when the new AA member is in a stronger and more stable position and with qualified people. This is particularly important to the newcomer or any member who has been avoiding taking an inventory due to fear or embarrassment.

Again, step 4 is not concerned with details of events as much as identifying self-centered character defects. In order to progress to the point where the alcoholic is able to address these much deeper issues, they must stay sober, and by addressing the self-centered character defects immediately, the new member is in a much stronger position to achieve sobriety.

Step 4 is not intended to uncover some hidden cause to our actions. Step 4 is solely used to identify self-centered patterns of behavior so that we know what to bring to our higher power in step 7. It is in taking step 7 that we seek our higher power's assistance in relieving us of our character defects, not the details of our troubles.

The details of our past are unimportant and likely distracting as far as step 4 is concerned. We cannot change our past actions. Our higher power cannot change our past actions. We can only change, with a higher power's help, our current behavior. Identifying what character defects are part of our pattern of behavior in the present time, and the harms they have caused, is the sole purpose of the 4th step.

Step 4 was never meant to be anything more than a LIST of character defects. In fact, from pages 64 to 70 in The Big Book, the word list or listed is used five times along with the phrases "we put them (our character defects) down on paper" and again "we got this all down on paper", referring to the specific character defects we are instructed to be looking for: resentment, fear, selfishness, dishonesty, pride, jealousy and bitterness (envy).

The inventory example in The Big Book has a list of names that one is resentful at, the cause, (the nature of the resentment) and what the character defect affected, (how did the character defect manifest?) with the understanding that we would do exactly the same thing with the other defects we are instructed to look for.

In Bill's Story, Bill describes taking step 4 with his sponsor, while still in a hospital; Bill states he and Ebby **"made a list of the people I had hurt or toward whom I felt resentment."**

The Big Book also states: "we treat sex as we would any other problem". We do not add a special category for sex; we simply find where the seven character defects have impacted our sexual relationships just as they have our other relationships.

Nowhere are we instructed to use worksheets attempting to identify an almost endless list of questionable behavior, which if looked at closely, are simply manifestations of the seven already mentioned. We are also not instructed to give a written narrative of our entire drinking history or every incidence of unpleasant or anti-social behavior. These are methods used by many people today and encouraged by many treatment centers, with the misguided notion that more is better.

No wonder these complicated and distracting methods appeal to the alcoholic ego. The sorry results of using these other methods is that very few alcoholics are ever able to achieve the comfortable, contented, useful and permanent sobriety that most AA members enjoyed 75 years ago.

Many in AA do not want to believe that step 4 could be as simple as making a list of people that we have harmed or had been resentful, fearful, selfish, dishonest, prideful, jealous, or envious with, but this is EXACTLY what The Big Book is directing us to do. Nothing more. In the checklist we use in this workshop, we have also added laziness, as laziness was included in the checklist that Dr. Bob used in taking over 5000 alcoholics through the steps. After all, weren't most of us lazy (procrastinating) when faced with taking responsibility for our actions?

As stated earlier, when AA members used the checklist method rather than a written narrative, we achieve a success rate of alcoholics maintaining their sobriety of over 50%. Many methods used today have made a once simple step very complicated. In our attempt to copy a psychological model, we have become less successful. Alcoholics, who were at one time offered a clear path to sobriety, now struggle to stay sober, and many die.

The simple and straightforward method of taking step 4 described in The Big Book and used in the Spiritual Solution Workshops is a proven and highly effective way of identifying what character defects have held us in bondage to self and to active addiction. These are precisely the character defects that hinder our recovery as they block us from a relationship with a higher power of our understanding, a higher or greater power that can relieve our alcoholism.

By identifying these specific character defects, we overcome the effects of self-centeredness leading to the alcoholic's devastating ability to remain blind to the effects of their behavior. This new-found awareness of these selfish patterns of behavior will finally provide us with the ability to identify how they manifest in our lives. With this awareness we have a clear understanding of what we ask our higher power to alleviate in prayer and meditation. We also will have a clear understanding of what to include in our daily 10th step inventories.

The fifth step asks us to admit to God, to ourselves, and to another human being, the exact NATURE of our wrongs; what specific character defect is at the root of our aberrant behavior? On page 62, paragraph 1, The Big Book authors write: "Selfishness, self-centeredness! That we think is the root of our troubles." On page 72, paragraph 1 they write "we have admitted CERTAIN defects". What certain defects? The eight previously mentioned, including laziness.

The Big Book Authors are certainly not directing us to write or talk endlessly about the minute details of our lives. The nature of our wrongs is what we have identified in step 4, our character defects, and when step 4 is taken with a sponsor or other sharing partner, we are taking step 5, admitting our wrongs to another human being at the same time. Note that we are directed to take step 5 with another human being, not necessarily our sponsor. If we do not actually take step 4 with our sponsor, it is best to review the step 4 checklist with them.

This is how early members took newcomers through steps 4 and 5. Newcomers were not directed to go off by themselves, still sick from the effects of alcoholism, and told to write their drunk-a-log or life story or every incidence of unpleasant or anti-social behavior. As sponsors we sat down with our sponsee and assisted them in completing their checklist, asking the appropriate questions as we went along. In this way, sponsors are able to keep their sponsee's focus on step 4, on uncovering their defects of character, without getting bogged down in the details of their lives.

As our co-founder Dr. Bob Smith instructed: **Keep It Simple.**

Step 4

Made a searching and fearless moral inventory of ourselves
(Steps 4 and 5 instructions begin after step 5 readings)

(13:3) My schoolmate visited me, and I fully acquainted him with my problems and deficiencies. **We made a list of people I had hurt or toward whom I felt resentment.** I expressed my entire willingness to approach these individuals, admitting my wrong. Never was I to be critical of them. I was to right all such matters to the utmost of my ability.

(63:4) Next we launched out on a course of vigorous action, the first step of which is a personal housecleaning, which many of us had never attempted. Though our decision was a vital and crucial step, it could have little permanent effect unless at once followed by a strenuous effort to face, and to be rid of, the things in ourselves which had been blocking us. Our liquor was but a symptom. So we had to get down to causes and conditions.

(64:1) **Therefore, we started upon a personal inventory. This was Step Four.** A business which takes no regular inventory usually goes broke. Taking a commercial inventory is a fact-finding and a fact-facing process. It is an effort to discover the truth about the stock-in-trade. One object is to disclose damaged or unsalable goods, to get rid of them promptly and without regret. If the owner of the business is to be successful, he cannot fool himself about values.

(64:2) We did exactly the same thing with our lives. We took stock honestly. First, we searched out the flaws in our make-up which caused our failure. Being convinced that self, manifested in various ways, was what had defeated us, we considered its common manifestations.

(64:3) Resentment is the "number one" offender. It destroys more alcoholics than anything else. From it stem all forms of spiritual disease, for we have been not only mentally and physically ill, we have been spiritually sick. When the spiritual malady is overcome, we straighten out mentally and physically. In dealing with resentments, we set them on paper. **We listed people, institutions or principles** with whom we were angry. We asked ourselves why we were angry. In most cases it was found that our self-esteem, our pocketbooks, our ambitions, our personal relationships (including sex) were hurt or threatened. So we were sore. We were "burned up."

(65:3) We went back through our lives. Nothing counted but thoroughness and honesty. When we were finished we considered it carefully. The first thing apparent was that this world and its people were often quite wrong. To conclude that others were wrong was as far as most of us ever got. The usual outcome was that people continued to wrong us and we stayed sore. Sometimes it was remorse and then we were sore at ourselves. But the more we fought and tried to have our own way, the worse matters got. As in war, the victor only seemed to win. Our moments of triumph were short-lived.

(66:1) It is plain that a life which includes deep resentment leads only to futility and unhappiness. To the precise extent that we permit these, do we squander the hours that might have been worth while. But with the alcoholic, whose hope is the maintenance and growth of a spiritual experience, this business of resentment is infinitely grave. We found that it is fatal. For when harboring such feelings we shut ourselves off from the sunlight of the Spirit. The insanity of alcohol returns and we drink again. And with us, to drink is to die.

(66:2) If we were to live, we had to be free of anger. The grouch and the brainstorm were not for us. They may be the dubious luxury of normal men, but for alcoholics these things are poison.

(66:3) **We turned back to the list, for it held the key to the future**. We were prepared to look at it from an entirely different angle. We began to see that the world and its people really dominated us. In that state, the wrong-doing of others, fancied or real, had power to actually kill. How could we escape? We saw that these resentments must be mastered, but how? We could not wish them away any more than alcohol.

(67:0) Though we did not like their symptoms and the way these disturbed us, they, like ourselves, were sick too. We asked God to help us show them the same tolerance, pity, and patience that we would cheerfully grant a sick friend. When a person offended we said to ourselves, "This is a sick man. How can I be helpful to him? God save me from being angry. Thy will be done."

(67:1) We avoid retaliation or argument. We wouldn't treat sick people that way. If we do, we destroy our chance of being helpful. We cannot be helpful to all people, but at least God will show us how to take a kindly and tolerant view of each and every one.

(67:2) **Referring to our list again.** Putting out of our minds the wrongs others had done, we resolutely looked for our own mistakes. Where had we been selfish, dishonest, self-seeking and frightened? Though a situation had not been entirely our fault, we tried to disregard the other person involved entirely. Where were we to blame? The inventory was ours, not the other man's. **When we saw our faults we listed them**. We placed them before us in black and white. We admitted our wrongs honestly and were willing to set these matters straight.

75

(68:1) We reviewed our fears thoroughly. We put them on paper, even though we had no resentment in connection with them. We asked ourselves why we had them. Wasn't it because self-reliance failed us? Self-reliance was good as far as it went, but it didn't go far enough. Some of us once had great self-confidence, but it didn't fully solve the fear problem, or any other. When it made us cocky, it was worse.

(68:2) Perhaps there is a better way - we think so. For we are now on a different basis; the basis of trusting and relying upon God. We trust infinite God rather than our finite selves. We are in the world to play the role He assigns. Just to the extent that we do as we think He would have us, and humbly rely on Him, does He enable us to match calamity with serenity.

(68:3) We never apologize to anyone for depending upon our Creator. We can laugh at those who think spirituality the way of weakness. Paradoxically, it is the way of strength. The verdict of the ages is that faith means courage. All men of faith have courage. They trust their God. We never apologize for God. Instead we let Him demonstrate, through us, what He can do. We ask Him to remove our fear and direct our attention to what He would have us be. At once, we commence to outgrow fear.

(69:1) We reviewed our own conduct over the years past. **Where had we been selfish, dishonest, or inconsiderate? Whom had we hurt? Did we unjustifiably arouse jealousy, suspicion or bitterness?** Where were we at fault, what should we have done instead? **We got this all down on paper and looked at it.**

Step 5

Admitted to God, to ourselves, and to another human being the exact nature of our wrongs

(72:1) Having made our personal inventory, what shall we do about it? We have been trying to get a new attitude, a new relationship with our Creator, and to discover the obstacles in our path. We have admitted certain defects; we have ascertained in a rough way what the trouble is; we have put our finger on the weak items in our personal inventory. Now these are about to be cast out. This requires action on our part, which, **when completed, will mean that we have admitted to God, to ourselves, and to another human being, the exact nature of our defects.** This brings us to the Fifth Step in the program of recovery mentioned in the preceding chapter.

(72:2) This is perhaps difficult - especially discussing our defects with another person. We think we have done well enough in admitting these things to ourselves. There is doubt about that. In actual practice, we usually find a solitary self-appraisal insufficient. Many of us thought it necessary to go much further. We will be more reconciled to discussing ourselves with another person when we see good reasons why we should do so. The best reason first: If we skip this vital step, we may not overcome drinking. Time after time newcomers have tried to keep to themselves certain facts about their lives. Trying to avoid this humbling experience, they have turned to easier methods.

(73:0) Almost invariably they got drunk. Having persevered with the rest of the program, they wondered why they fell. We think the reason is that they never completed their housecleaning. They took inventory all right, but hung on to some of the worst items in stock. They only thought they had lost their egoism and fear; they only thought they had humbled themselves. But they had not learned enough of humility, fearlessness and honesty, in the sense we find it necessary, until they told someone else all their life story.

(73:1) More than most people, the alcoholic leads a double life. He is very much the actor. To the outer world he presents his stage character. This is the one he likes his fellows to see. He wants to enjoy a certain reputation, but knows in his heart he doesn't deserve it.

(73:2) The inconsistency is made worse by the things he does on his sprees. Coming to his senses, he is revolted at certain episodes he vaguely remembers. These memories are a nightmare. He trembles to think someone might have observed him. As fast as he can, he pushes these memories far inside himself. He hopes they will never see the light of day. He is under constant fear and tension - that makes for more drinking.

(73:3) Psychologists are inclined to agree with us. We have spent thousands of dollars for examinations. We know but few instances where we have given these doctors a fair break. We have seldom told them the whole truth nor have we followed their advice. Unwilling to be honest with these sympathetic men, we were honest with no one else. Small wonder many in the medical profession have a low opinion of alcoholics and their chance for recovery!

(73:4) We must be entirely honest with somebody if we expect to live long or happily in this world. Rightly and naturally, we think well before we choose the person or persons with whom to take this intimate and confidential

78

step. Those of us belonging to a religious denomination which requires confession must, and of course, will want to go to the properly appointed authority whose duty it is to receive it. Though we have no religious connection, we may still do well to talk with someone ordained by an established religion. We often find such a person quick to see and understand our problem. Of course, we sometimes encounter people who do not understand alcoholics.

(75:1) When we decide who is to hear our story, we waste no time. We have a written inventory and we are prepared for a long talk. We explain to our partner what we are about to do and why we have to do it. He should realize that we are engaged upon a life-and-death errand. Most people approached in this way will be glad to help; they will be honored by our confidence.

(75:2) We pocket our pride and go to it, illuminating every twist of character, every dark cranny of the past. Once we have taken this step, withholding nothing, we are delighted. We can look the world in the eye. We can be alone at perfect peace and ease. Our fears fall from us. We begin to feel the nearness of our Creator. We may have had certain spiritual beliefs, but now we begin to have a spiritual experience. The feeling that the drink problem has disappeared will often come strongly. We feel we are on the Broad Highway, walking hand in hand with the Spirit of the Universe.

(75:3) Returning home we find a place where we can be quiet for an hour, carefully reviewing what we have done. We thank God from the bottom of our heart that we know Him better. Taking this book down from our shelf we turn to the page which contains the twelve steps. Carefully reading the first five proposals we ask if we have omitted anything, for we are building an arch through which we shall walk a free man at last. Is our work solid so far? Are the stones properly in place? Have we skimped on the cement put into the foundation? Have we tried to make mortar without sand?

(164:3) Abandon yourself to God as you understand God. Admit your faults to Him and to your fellows. Clear away the wreckage of your past. Give freely of what you find and join us. We shall be with you in the Fellowship of the Spirit, and you will surely meet some of us as you trudge the Road of Happy Destiny.

Steps 4 and 5 Instructions

The step 4 inventory list will clearly show the aspects of our behavior that **at this point in our lives** block us from a manageable life and from loving relationships with those around us. Most importantly, these "character defects" block us from a relationship to a higher power of our understanding. These self-centered character defects are clearly listed on pages 64 to 71 of The Big Book as resentment, fear, dishonesty, inconsideration (pride), jealousy, and bitterness (envy). As previously mentioned, step 4 is not meant to be a drunk-a-log or an exhaustive list of every incidence of unpleasant behavior over the course of our lives. A correct step 4 will clearly establish a pattern of self-centered behavior that we as alcoholics adopted to enable us to live lives as active alcoholics and keep us isolated from others and a higher power.

The Big Book authors use as a step 4 analogy a business taking an inventory. When a business performs an inventory, they are concerned with their assets and liabilities **at the present moment.** There is no value to the business to recollect what was on hand twenty years prior. Also, the entire history of the company is not reviewed in minute detail in order for the company to perform an effective inventory. This would be a waste of time and effort, and ultimately, a distraction from what they are trying to accomplish: identifying their liabilities so that they can eliminate them, and, as important, identifying their assets so that they know what they have to build their future on.

We are doing the same thing. We want to identify our liabilities so that we can give them to our higher power, and we want to discover what our assets are so that with our higher power's assistance we can use them as the foundation for our sober lives.

Identifying these defects and the harms we have caused is the SOLE purpose of the fourth step. It is a fearless and thorough moral INVENTORY - what is our behavior right now, who have we harmed, what are our fears, and how do these character defects manifest in our lives. The definition of inventory is "a detailed list." By listing our self-centered character defects we are finally able to overcome the alcoholics devastating ability to remain blind to patterns of behavior which would otherwise lead back to active alcoholism. This new awareness of self is the beginning of God-consciousness.

We will use the checklist provided and we will each have a sharing partner to review this step with. If you are more comfortable being "generic" regarding specific people, institutions, etc., simply use first names or initials. What is most important is to establish a pattern of behavior and identify harms done.

The sponsor or sharing partner does the writing, asking the appropriate questions and filling in the inventory checklist. (Checklist example is on page 89) A good way to start is to list all people that are most important to you and that you interact with on a daily basis including immediate family, co-workers and close friends, whether you have "resentments" or not with these people. Then ask yourself who would you not want to walk into this room and sit down next to you. Whom do you avoid facing? List these people. Next, list who you have strong negative feelings about and what people or situations are occupying much of your thinking. Do the same with businesses and/or institutions.

Once you have created your list of people, review the Step 4 Inventory Definitions in the next chapter.

Beginning with the first person on your list, the sponsor or sharing partner asks if there is any resentment in the relationship. If not, move on to fear, etc.

Notice that a resentment is a "hostile, indignant, or contemptuous attitude" we are holding against someone. It is important to be clear that what we are harboring is in fact resentment and not just some vague feeling of disappointment with someone. The point is that our resentment has actually affected the relationship in some negative way.

If there are resentments affecting this relationship, put a check in the appropriate box. Then the sponsor or sharing partner will ask "what is the nature of the resentment, how has the resentment manifested in this relationship and how has it affected the relationship? Has a harm been done?"

If a harm has been done, cross the check as an indication that an amends needs to be made. A harm is something that has caused someone actual suffering or loss, something that we have done that has had a negative effect on another.

Once you have looked at resentment, move on to fear, again asking what is the nature of the fear, how did it manifest in the relationship and how has it affected the relationship? Was any harm done?

Continue with the rest of the checklist putting a check as appropriate until the inventory is completed for the first person. Do the same with the remaining people and institutions on the list. Not everyone on the list will have checks and in some cases there may be very few "liabilities". Many people realize after an inventory has been completed that they are not as "bad" as they thought. We are not bad people trying to be good, we are sick people trying to get well.

Taking an extremely harsh view of ourselves, thinking that we are worse than we really are, and that our behavior has had a deep and profound effect on others can also be characteristic of self-centeredness and false pride. None of us are unique in our behavior or in our drinking and/or drugging.

Once the inventory is complete, you will have a clear picture of your patterns of behavior and harms done, and a clear understanding of what you will seek a higher power's assistance with in step 7.

THE SPIRITUAL SOLUTION

Remember that you are also making your eighth step list at this time.

The assets that are on the bottom of the columns are what we are striving to incorporate into our new personalities, and when we act in this way, we are acting in accordance with God's will for us. If we have resentments in our lives, we will strive for forgiveness. If we find we have fear in our lives, it is clear that we need to develop faith, if we are acting in a dishonest way, we strive for honesty, etc.

When you have completed the list and discussed the list with your sharing partner, take time to quietly review the list with your higher power. Thank your Higher Power their continued support in developing comfortable and contented sobriety. You are well on your way to fitting yourself to be of service to others with this disease.

Upon completion of your written inventory, sharing with your sponsor or sharing partner, and having reviewed your list with your higher power, you have completed Steps 4 and 5. Once you have completed this, reverse roles with the sharing partner now taking this step. The one who has just taken the 4th and 5th will now do the writing and acting as sharing partner.

If during this fourth step inventory it is found that more discussion is needed to find relief from severe trauma or long-hidden misdeeds, seek the further assistance of a qualified sponsor and also consider a qualified therapist. Remember that none of us as sponsors or sharing partners are counselors or therapists and it is not the intent of the 12 Steps to address every possible psychological or emotional problem. Step 4 is only meant to uncover manifestations of self-centered behavior.

From page 64, paragraph 2 of The Big Book: "...we searched out the flaws in our make-up, which caused our failure. **Being convinced that self, manifested in various ways, was what had defeated us, we considered its common manifestations.**"

84

Remember that this will not be your last fourth and fifth step. Hopefully taking the steps and taking others through the steps will become a regular part of your sobriety.

Step 4 Inventory Definitions

Liabilities (Self Will)

Resentment: a feeling of deep and bitter anger and ill-will, a feeling of anger or displeasure stemming from belief that others have engaged in wrongdoing or mistreatment; dismissive, contemptuous; a hostile or indignant attitude. Resentment directed at self is remorse.

Fear: anxiety or apprehension about a possible or probable situation or event, fear is an emotional response to a perceived threat, afraid of losing something we have or not getting something we want. Phobia, panic, terror, anxiety and worry are all manifestations of fear. Fear is finding fault with the future.

Selfishness: placing one's own needs or desires above the needs or well being of others, an excessive concern for your own welfare and a disregard of others.

Dishonesty: acts of lying, cheating or stealing, being deliberately deceptive, lacking in integrity, taking what does not belong to us.

Pride/False Pride: Pride is thinking that one is superior to others in some way. Pride is presenting yourself to others (and yourself) as something you are not - a person without flaws, prejudice, and arrogance. Feeling less than others is false pride as it arises from a pre-occupation with self, as does dwelling on self-pity and self-doubt and maintaining a lack of self worth. Both extremes of pride/false pride are rooted in a lack of humility - knowing who you truly are.

Jealousy: negative thoughts and feelings of insecurity, suspicion, fear and anxiety over an anticipated loss of something that you value, such as a relationship, friendship or love. distrust, mistrust, possessiveness

Envy: spite and resentment at seeing the success of another, wanting another's possessions.

Laziness: inactivity resulting from a dislike of work or accomplishment, procrastination is a form of laziness, not doing what is in one's best interest or what is expected of us.

Assets (God's Will)

Forgiveness: complete acceptance of another's perceived faults or wrongdoings, being free of judgments.

Faith/Love: a sincere belief in God's will, an unselfish and benevolent concern for another's well-being, love extends oneself for the purpose of nurturing another's spiritual growth.

Unselfishness: a strong intention to serve, generousness, generosity of spirit, to give freely.

Honesty: adherence to the truth.

Humility: acceptance of self as one is, being modest, down to earth, equal to all others.

Trust: confidence, faith in other's intentions.

Contentment: being at peace with the people and events of one's life, a deep satisfaction with one's life as it is.

Action: doing what is needed or indicated without delay.

Step 4 Sample Inventory Checklist

This sample inventory is an example only. The 4th step inventory checklist used during the Spiritual Solution Workshops is available for free download at
www.johnh12steps.com

Name	Resentment	Fear	Selfish	Dishonest	Pride	Jealous	Envy	Lazy
Spouse	✓	✓				✓		
Boss	✗			✗			✓	
Bank	✓			✗				
Higher Power								
Self								
AA	✓							
	Forgiveness	Faith	Selfless	Honest	Humble	Trust	Content	Action

In this sample inventory there are resentments with the spouse, the boss, the bank and AA. Amends will need to be made to the boss for actions caused by resentment and additional amends to the boss and the bank for dishonesty - note the cross checks.

Character defects arose as fear, jealousy and envy as well.

As can be seen, by using a checklist, patterns of behavior are quickly apparent and harms done rising to the level of making an amends necessary are also apparent.

The liabilities are caused by acting out of self-will and our assets become apparent when acting in accordance with God's will. As we learn to identify patterns of behavior, we will also learn behavior that is more appropriate. For instance, if we see a pattern of resentment it is clear we need to strive for forgiveness. If we identify fear, we will strive for faith and love. If we exhibit laziness, we will begin to take appropriate action, etc.

Step 6

Were entirely ready to have God remove all these defects of character

(75:3) Returning home we find a place where we can be quiet for an hour, carefully reviewing what we have done. We thank God from the bottom of our heart that we know Him better. Taking this book down from our shelf we turn to the page which contains the twelve steps. Carefully reading the first five proposals we ask if we have omitted anything, for we are building an arch through which we shall walk a free man at last. Is our work solid so far? Are the stones properly in place? Have we skimped on the cement put into the foundation? Have we tried to make mortar without sand?

(76:1) If we can answer to our satisfaction, we then look at Step Six. We have emphasized willingness as being indispensable. **Are we now ready to let God remove from us all the things which we have admitted are objectionable?** Can He now take them all - every one? If we still cling to something we will not let go, we ask God to help us be willing.

Step 6 asks us if we are ready to have the God of our understanding remove those character defects that we developed as active alcoholics, and if not removed, will lead back to drinking.

If you think you are not "entirely" ready, when will you be? Some of us will be hung up on the words "entirely ready" and

91

feel the need to analyze the word "entirely". The only meaningful question is if you are not ready for comfortable, contented sobriety now, when will you be?

~ ~ ~

Taking Step 6: (the group stands and individually answers)

Are you now ready to let God remove from you all the things which you have admitted are objectionable?

If you can answer yes, you have taken Step 6.

~ ~ ~

Step 7

Humbly asked Him to remove our shortcomings

(76:2) When ready, we say something like this: **"My Creator, I am now willing that you should have all of me, good and bad. I pray that you now remove from me every single defect of character which stands in the way of my usefulness to you and my fellows. Grant me strength, as I go out from here, to do your bidding. Amen."** We have then completed Step Seven.

Step 7 is an affirming prayer. We have now identified those aspects of our character, our "defects", which have kept us addicted to alcohol and dis-connected from a higher power. More than likely, some of our poor behavior will remain for some time. Taking step 7 will bring a new awareness of how these character defects manifest in our lives.

Through continuing to incorporate the remaining five steps, making amends where needed, taking a daily inventory, daily prayer and meditation, and working with others, our very lives will become the answer to the seventh step prayer. We will have a new awareness of self and our place in the world. This new awareness is the beginning of God-consciousness.

We will now have the ability to make more skillful decisions and take actions that are more appropriate. Our higher power will use this new awareness of self as the means for healing. We will soon be able to experience the release from bondage of self and the realization of the promises of sobriety!

~ ~ ~

Taking Step 7: (Group recites prayer)

"My creator, I am now willing that you should have all of me, good and bad. I pray that you now remove from me every single defect of character which stands in the way of my usefulness to you and my fellows. Grant me strength as I go out from here to do your bidding. Amen."

When you have sincerely said this prayer, you have taken Step 7.

~ ~ ~

Step 8

Made a list of all persons we had harmed, and became willing to make amends to them all

(69:3) Whatever our ideal turns out to be, we must be willing to grow toward it. We must be willing to make amends where we have done harm, provided that we do not bring about still more harm in so doing. In other words, we treat sex as we would any other problem. In meditation, we ask God what we should do about each specific matter. The right answer will come, if we want it.

(76:3) Now we need more action, without which we find that "Faith without works is dead." Let's look at Steps Eight and Nine. **We have a list of all persons we have harmed and to whom we are willing to make amends. We made it when we took inventory.** We subjected ourselves to a drastic self-appraisal. Now we go out to our fellows and repair the damage done in the past. We attempt to sweep away the debris which has accumulated out of our effort to live on self-will and run the show ourselves. If we have not the will to do this, we ask until it comes. Remember it was agreed at the beginning *we would go to any lengths for victory over alcohol.*

We have a step 8 amends list from step 4. If you are not now willing to continue and follow through with your amends, again ask your self when will you be ready for comfortable, contented sobriety and continued growth along spiritual lines.

Using the third and seventh steps prayers are an effective way of reinforcing our willingness to continue with the program of recovery.

~ ~ ~

Taking Step 8: You made a list when you wrote your 4th step inventory. Beginning your ninth step amends affirms your continued willingness.

~ ~ ~

Step 9

Made direct amends to such people wherever possible, except when to do so would injure them or others

(76:3) **Now we go out to our fellows and repair the damage done in the past. We attempt to sweep away the debris which has accumulated out of our effort to live on self-will and run the show ourselves.** If we haven't the will to do this, we ask until it comes. Remember it was agreed at the beginning *we would go to any lengths for victory over alcohol.*

(76:4) Probably there are still some misgivings. As we look over the list of business acquaintances and friends we have hurt, we may feel diffident about going to some of them on a spiritual basis. Let us be reassured. To some people we need not, and probably should not emphasize the spiritual feature on our first approach.

(77:0) We might prejudice them. At the moment we are trying to put our lives in order. But this is not an end in itself. **Our real purpose is to fit ourselves to be of maximum service to God and the people about us.** It is seldom wise to approach an individual, who still smarts from our injustice to him, and announce that we have gone religious. In the prize ring, this would be called leading with the chin. Why lay ourselves open to being branded fanatics or religious bores? We may kill a future opportunity to carry a beneficial message. But our man is sure to be impressed with a sincere desire to set right the wrong. He is going to be more interested in a demonstration of good will than in our talk of spiritual discoveries.

(77:1) We don't use this as an excuse for shying away from the subject of God. When it will serve any good purpose, we are willing to announce our convictions with tact and common sense. The question of how to approach the man we hated will arise. It may be he has done us more harm than we have done him and, though we may have acquired a better attitude toward him, we are still not too keen about admitting our faults. Nevertheless, with a person we dislike, we take the bit in our teeth. It is harder to go to an enemy than to a friend, but we find it much more beneficial to us. We go to him in a helpful and forgiving spirit, confessing our former ill feeling and expressing our regret.

(77:2) Under no condition do we criticize such a person or argue. Simply we tell him that we will never get over drinking until we have done our utmost to straighten out the past. We are there to sweep off our side of the street, realizing that nothing worth while can be accomplished until we do so, never trying to tell him what he should do. His faults are not discussed. We stick to our own. If our manner is calm, frank, and open, we will be gratified with the result.

(78:1) In nine cases out of ten the unexpected happens. Sometimes the man we are calling upon admits his own fault, so feuds of years' standing melt away in an hour. Rarely do we fail to make satisfactory progress. Our former enemies sometimes praise what we are doing and wish us well. Occasionally, they will offer assistance. It should not matter, however, if someone does throw us out of his office. We have made our demonstration, done our part. It's water over the dam.

(78:2) Most alcoholics owe money. We do not dodge our creditors. Telling them what we are trying to do, we make no bones about our drinking; they usually know it anyway, whether we think so or not. Nor are we afraid of disclosing our alcoholism on the theory it may cause financial harm. Approached in this way, the most ruthless creditor will sometimes surprise us. Arranging the best deal we can we let these people know we are sorry. Our drinking has made us slow to pay. We must lose our fear of creditors no matter how far we have to go, for we are liable to drink if we are afraid to face them.

(78:3) Perhaps we have committed a criminal offense which might land us in jail if it were known to the authorities. We may be short in our accounts and unable to make good. We have already admitted this in confidence to another person, but we are sure we would be imprisoned or lose our job if it were known. Maybe it's only a petty offense such as padding the expense account. Most of us have done that sort of thing.

(79:0 Maybe we are divorced, and have remarried but haven't kept up the alimony to number one. She is indignant about it, and has a warrant out for our arrest. That's a common form of trouble too.

(79:1) Although these reparations take innumerable forms, there are some general principles which we find guiding. Reminding ourselves that we have decided to go to any lengths to find a spiritual experience, we ask that we be given strength and direction to do the right thing, no matter what the personal consequences may be. We may lose our position or reputation or face jail, but we are willing. We have to be. We must not shrink at anything.

(79:2) Usually, however, other people are involved. Therefore, we are not to be the hasty and foolish martyr who would needlessly sacrifice others to save himself from the alcoholic pit. A man we know had remarried. Because of resentment and drinking, he had not paid alimony to his first wife. She was furious. She went to court and got an order for his arrest. He had commenced our way of life, had secured a position, and was getting his

99

head above water. It would have been impressive heroics if he had walked up to the Judge and said, "Here I am."

(79:3) We thought he ought to be willing to do that if necessary, but if he were in jail he could provide nothing for either family. We suggested he write his first wife admitting his faults and asking forgiveness. He did, and also sent a small amount of money. He told her what he would try to do in the future. He said he was perfectly willing to go to jail if she insisted. Of course she did not, and the whole situation has long since been adjusted.

(80:1) Before taking drastic action which might implicate other people we secure their consent. If we have obtained permission, have consulted with others, asked God to help and the drastic step is indicated we must not shrink.

(80:2) This brings to mind a story about one of our friends. While drinking, he accepted a sum of money from a bitterly-hated business rival, giving him no receipt for it. He subsequently denied having received the money and used the incident as a basis for discrediting the man. He thus used his own wrong-doing as a means of destroying the reputation of another. In fact, his rival was ruined.

(80:3) He felt that he had done a wrong he could not possibly make right. If he opened that old affair, he was afraid it would destroy the reputation of his partner, disgrace his family and take away his means of livelihood. What right had he to involve those dependent upon him? How could he possibly make a public statement exonerating his rival?

(80:4) After consulting with his wife and partner he came to the conclusion that is was better to take those risks than to stand before his Creator guilty of such ruinous slander. He saw that he had to place the outcome in God's hands or he would soon start drinking again, and all would be lost anyhow. He attended church for the first time in many years. After the sermon, he quietly got up and made an explanation. His action met wide-spread approval, and today he is one of the most trusted citizens of his town. This all happened years ago.

(80:5) The chances are that we have domestic troubles. Perhaps we are mixed up with women in a fashion we wouldn't care to have advertised. We doubt if, in this respect, alcoholics are fundamentally much worse than other people. But drinking does complicate sex relations in the home. After a few years with an alcoholic, a wife gets worn out, resentful and uncommunicative. How could she be anything else? The husband begins to feel lonely, sorry for himself. He commences to look around in the night clubs, or their equivalent, for something besides liquor. Perhaps he is having a secret and exciting affair with "the girl who understands." In fairness we must say that she may understand, but what are we going to do about a thing like that? A man so involved often feels very remorseful at times, especially if he is married to a loyal and courageous girl who has literally gone through hell for him.

(81:1) Whatever the situation, we usually have to do something about it. If we are sure our wife does not know, should we tell her? Not always, we think. If she knows in a general way that we have been wild, should we tell her in detail? Undoubtedly we should admit our fault. She may insist on knowing all the particulars. She will want to know who the woman is and where she is. We feel we ought to say to her that we have no right to involve another person. We are sorry for what we have done and, God willing, it shall not be repeated. More than that we cannot do; we have no right to go further. Though there may be justifiable exceptions, and though we wish to lay down no rule of any sort, we have often found this the best course to take.

(81:2) Our design for living is not a one-way street. It is as good for the wife as for the husband. If we can forget, so can she. It is better, however, that one does not needlessly name a person upon whom she can vent jealousy.

(82:1) Perhaps there are some cases where the utmost frankness is demanded. No outsider can appraise such an intimate situation. It may be that both will decide that the way of good sense and loving kindness is to let bygones be bygones. Each might pray about it, having the other one's happiness uppermost in mind. Keep it always in sight that we are dealing with that most terrible human emotion-jealousy. Good generalship may decide that the problem be attacked on the flank rather than risk a face-to-face combat.

(82:2) If we have no such complication, there is plenty we should do at home. Sometimes we hear an alcoholic say that the only thing he needs to do is to keep sober. Certainly he must keep sober, for there will be no home if he doesn't. But he is yet a long way from making good to the wife or parents whom for years he has so shockingly treated. Passing all understanding is the patience mothers and wives have had with alcoholics. Had this not been so, many of us would have no homes today, would perhaps be dead.

(82:3) The alcoholic is like a tornado roaring his way through the lives of others. Hearts are broken. Sweet relationships are dead. Affections have been uprooted. Selfish and inconsiderate habits have kept the home in turmoil. We feel a man is unthinking when he says that sobriety is enough. He is like the farmer who came up out of his cyclone cellar to find his home ruined. To his wife, he remarked, "Don't see anything the matter here, Ma. Ain't it grand the wind stopped blowin'?"

(83:1) Yes, there is a long period of reconstruction ahead. We must take the lead. A remorseful mumbling that we are sorry won't fill the bill at all. We ought to sit down with the family and frankly analyze the past as we now see it, being very careful not to criticize them. Their defects may be glaring, but the chances are that our own actions are partly responsible. So we clean house with the family, asking each morning in meditation that our Creator show us the way of patience, tolerance, kindliness and love.

(83:2) **The spiritual life is not a theory. We have to live it.** Unless one's family expresses a desire to live upon spiritual principles we think we ought not to urge them. We should not talk incessantly to them about spiritual matters. They will change in time. Our behavior will convince them more than our words. We must remember that ten or twenty years of drunkenness would make a skeptic out of anyone.

(83:3) There may be some wrongs we can never fully right. We don't worry about them if we can honestly say to ourselves that we would right them if we could. Some people cannot be seen - we send them an honest letter. And there may be a valid reason for postponement in some cases. But we don't delay if it can be avoided. We should be sensible, tactful, considerate and humble without being servile or scraping. As God's people we stand on our feet; we don't crawl before anyone.

(83:4) **If we are painstaking about this phase of our development, we will be amazed before we are half way through. We are going to know a new freedom and a new happiness. We will not regret the past nor wish to shut the door on it. We will comprehend the word serenity and we will know peace. No matter how far down the scale we have gone, we will see how our experience can benefit others. That feeling of uselessness and self-pity will disappear. We will lose interest in selfish things and gain interest in our fellows. Self-seeking will slip away. Our whole attitude and outlook upon life will change. Fear of people and of economic insecurity will leave us. We will intuitively know how to handle situations which used to baffle us.**

We will suddenly realize that God is doing for us what we could not do for ourselves.

(84:1) Are these extravagant promises? We think not. They are being fulfilled among us - sometimes quickly, sometimes slowly. They will always materialize if we work for them.

(156:1) (From Dr. Bob's story) One morning he took the bull by the horns and set out to tell those he feared what his trouble had been. He found himself surprisingly well received, and learned that many knew of his drinking. Stepping into his car, he made the rounds of people he had hurt. He trembled as he went about, for this might mean ruin, particularly to a person in his line of business.

(156:2) At midnight he came home exhausted, but very happy. **He has not had a drink since.** As we shall see, he now means a great deal to his community, and the major liabilities of thirty years of hard drinking have been repaired in four.

Making Amends

We now have our amends list and are ready and willing to continue to heal and to grow along spiritual lines. Steps 10, 11 and 12 will offer great support while making amends. By continuing with personal inventory we will be aware of any self-centered behavior that arises during our amends. Much strength and guidance will come from daily prayer and meditation.

Often, the most significant amends, certainly to those that love us the most, will be our continued sobriety. To those that love us the most and who we love the most it may seem that a sincere apology is not necessary. A sincere apology is often dismissed by many in AA today. A sincere apology, acknowledging our self-centered action, any harm it may have caused, and our strong intention to no longer act in this manner is the essence of Step 9. These are the amends that should be done immediately as the support of those closest to us will be a great support as we continue to practice the principles of this new spiritual life.

Many of us owe money or other property. Financial amends often take careful planning and preparation and the planning and preparation is part of the amends process. Using personal inventory and prayer and meditation to be certain we are not being dishonest, selfish, fearful or lazy (procrastinating), begin to make these amends as soon as possible as well. Discuss how to appropriately approach the individuals or institutions you will be making restitution to with your sponsor, if further guidance is needed.

Step 9 can be a difficult and unpleasant step but a crucial step. As soon as we begin to set right the harms we have caused, we begin to loose the bonds of self-centered behavior. We truly do begin to experience "a new freedom and a new happiness". Proceed wisely and immediately with the amends process and continue walking in the "sunlight of the spirit."

~ ~ ~

Commit to begin making amends immediately with the support of your sponsor based on the guidelines that we have reviewed.

Taking Step 9: (the group stands and individually answers) Will you begin to make amends this coming week?

If you answer yes you have begun to take Step 9.

~ ~ ~

Step 10

Continued to take personal inventory and when we were wrong promptly admitted it

(84:1) Are these extravagant promises? We think not. They are being fulfilled among us - sometimes quickly, sometimes slowly. They will always materialize if we work for them.

(84:2) **This thought brings us to *Step Ten*, which suggests we continue to take personal inventory and continue to set right any new mistakes as we go along.** We vigorously commenced this way of living as we cleaned up the past. We have entered the world of the Spirit. Our next function is to grow in understanding and effectiveness. This is not an overnight matter. It should continue for our lifetime. Continue to watch for selfishness, dishonesty, resentment, and fear. When these crop up, we ask God at once to remove them. We discuss them with someone immediately and make amends quickly if we have harmed anyone. Then we resolutely turn our thoughts to someone we can help. Love and tolerance of others is our code.

(84:3) And we have ceased fighting anything or anyone - even alcohol. For by this time sanity will have returned. We will seldom be interested in liquor. If tempted, we recoil from it as from a hot flame. We react sanely and normally, and we will find that this has happened automatically. We will see that our new attitude toward liquor has been given us without any thought or effort on our part. It just comes! That is the miracle of it. We are not fighting it, neither are we avoiding temptation. We feel as though we had been placed in a position of neutrality - safe and protected. We have not even sworn off. Instead, the problem has been removed. It does not exist for us. We are neither cocky nor are we afraid. That is our experience. That is how we react so long as we keep in fit spiritual condition.

(85:1) It is easy to let up on the spiritual program of action and rest on our laurels. We are headed for trouble if we do, for alcohol is a subtle foe. We are not cured of alcoholism. What we really have is a daily reprieve contingent on the maintenance of our spiritual condition. Every day is a day when we must carry the vision of God's will into all of our activities. "How can I best serve Thee - Thy will (not mine) be done." These are thoughts which must go with us constantly. We can exercise our will power along this line all we wish. It is the proper use of the will.

(85:2) Much has already been said about receiving strength, inspiration, and direction from Him who has all knowledge and power. If we have carefully followed directions, we have begun to sense the flow of His Spirit into us. To some extent we have become God-conscious. We have begun to develop this vital sixth sense.

(86:1) When we retire at night, we constructively review our day. Were we resentful, selfish, dishonest or afraid? Do we owe an apology? Have we kept something to ourselves which should be discussed with another person at once? Were we kind and loving toward all? What could we have done better? Were we thinking of ourselves most of the time? Or were we thinking of what we could do for others, of what we could pack into the stream of life? But we must be careful not to drift into worry, remorse or morbid reflection, for that would diminish our usefulness to others.

The tenth step inventory and the prayer and meditation of the eleventh step are meant to be a part of our daily spiritual practice as our way of keeping in fit spiritual condition.

The fourth step inventory checklist is very useful for conducting the tenth step inventory. Discuss your inventories with your sponsor. Do not forget to list all of the positive aspects of your behavior and your life as well. By doing this daily, you are continuing to take this step.

~ ~ ~

Taking Step 10: (the group stands and individually answers)

Will you continue to take a personal inventory and continue to set right any new mistakes as you go along?

If you can answer yes, you have now begun taking Step 10.

~ ~ ~

Step 11

Sought through prayer and meditation to improve our conscious contact with God as we understood Him, praying only for knowledge of His will for us and the power to carry that out

(85:3) **Step Eleven suggests prayer and meditation.** We shouldn't be shy on this matter of prayer. Better men than we are using it constantly. It works, if we have the proper attitude and work at it. It would be easy to be vague about this matter. Yet, we believe we can make some definite and valuable suggestions.

(86:1) After making our review we ask God's forgiveness and inquire what corrective measures should be taken.

(86:2) On awakening let us think about the twenty-four hours ahead. We consider our plans for the day. Before we begin, we ask God to direct our thinking, especially asking that it be divorced from self-pity, dishonest or self-seeking motives. Under these conditions we can employ our mental faculties with assurance, for after all God gave us brains to use. Our thought-life will be placed on a much higher plane when our thinking is cleared of wrong motives.

(86:3) In thinking about our day we may face indecision. We may not be able to determine which course to take. Here we ask God for inspiration, an intuitive thought or a decision. We relax and take it easy. We don't struggle. We are often surprised how the right answers come after we have tried this for a while.

(87:0) What used to be the hunch or the occasional inspiration gradually becomes a working part of the mind. Being still inexperienced and having just made conscious contact with God, it is not probable that we are going to be inspired at all times. We might pay for this presumption in all sorts of absurd actions and ideas. Nevertheless, we find that our thinking will, as time passes, be more and more on the plane of inspiration. We come to rely upon it.

(87:1) We usually conclude the period of meditation with a prayer that we be shown all through the day what our next step is to be, that we be given whatever we need to take care of such problems. We ask especially for freedom from self-will, and are careful to make no request for ourselves only. We may ask for ourselves, however, if others will be helped. We are careful never to pray for our own selfish ends. Many of us have wasted a lot of time doing that and it doesn't work. You can easily see why.

(87:2) If circumstances warrant, we ask our wives or friends to join us in morning meditation. If we belong to a religious denomination which requires a definite morning devotion, we attend to that also. If not members of religious bodies, we sometimes select and memorize a few set prayers which emphasize the principles we have been discussing. There are many helpful books also. Suggestions about these may be obtained from one's priest, minister, or rabbi. Be quick to see where religious people are right. Make use of what they offer.

(87:3) As we go through the day we pause, when agitated or doubtful, and ask for the right thought or action. We constantly remind ourselves we are no longer running the show, humbly saying to ourselves many times each day "Thy will be done." We are then in much less danger of excitement, fear, anger, worry, self-pity, or foolish decisions. We become much more efficient. We do

112

not tire so easily, for we are not burning up energy foolishly as we did when we were trying to arrange life to suit ourselves.

(88:1) It works - it really does. We alcoholics are undisciplined. So we let God discipline us in the simple way we have just outlined. But this is not all. There is action and more action. "Faith without works is dead."

Set aside time every day, twice a day, for a period of prayer and mediation. In prayer ask for the knowledge of your higher power's will for you and the power to carry that out. Review your behavior, taking note of manifestations of self-centeredness. If an amends is needed, do so immediately.

Take time in quiet solitude, focusing on your breath, relaxing in the presence of your true self/higher power. Do not be engaged by your thoughts during your meditation. As thoughts arise, simply and gently let your thoughts go and return your attention to your breath.

By doing this daily, you are taking steps 10 and 11. There are many informative books on meditation, and many effective teachers as well. You may want to further your spiritual practice by reading additional material and finding a teacher or spiritual advisor.

~ ~ ~

Taking Step 11: (the group stands and individually answers)

Will you pray and meditate daily?

If you answer yes, you have begun taking Step 11.

~ ~ ~

Step 12

Having had a spiritual awakening as the result of these steps, we tried to carry this message to alcoholics, and to practice these principles in all our affairs

(89:1) **Practical experience shows that nothing will so much insure immunity from drinking as intensive work with other alcoholics. It works when other activities fail. This is our** *twelfth suggestion*: **Carry this message to other alcoholics! You can help when no one else can. You can secure their confidence when others fail. Remember they are very ill.**

(89:2) Life will take on new meaning. To watch people recover, to see them help others, to watch loneliness vanish, to see a fellowship grow up about you, to have a host of friends - this is an experience you must not miss. We know you will not want to miss it. Frequent contact with newcomers and with each other is the bright spot of our lives.

(91:3) See your man alone, if possible. At first engage in general conversation. After a while, turn the talk to some phase of drinking. Tell him enough about your drinking habits, symptoms, and experiences to encourage him to speak of himself. If he wishes to talk, let him do so. You will thus get a better idea of how you ought to proceed. If he is not communicative, give him a sketch of your drinking career up to the time you quit. But say nothing, for the moment, of how that was accomplished. If he is in a serious mood dwell on the troubles liquor has caused you, being careful not to moralize or lecture. If his mood is light, tell him humorous stories of your escapades. Get him to tell some of his.

(91:4) When he sees you know all about the drinking game, commence to describe yourself as an alcoholic.

(92:0) Tell him how baffled you were, how you finally learned that you were sick. Give him an account of the struggles you made to stop. Show him the mental twist which leads to the first drink of a spree. We suggest you do this as we have done it in the chapter on alcoholism. If he is alcoholic, he will understand you at once. He will match your mental inconsistencies with some of his own.

(92:1) If you are satisfied that he is a real alcoholic, begin to dwell on the hopeless feature of the malady. Show him, from your own experience, how the queer mental condition surrounding that first drink prevents normal functioning of the will power. Don't, at this stage, refer to this book, unless he has seen it and wishes to discuss it. And be careful not to brand him as an alcoholic. Let him draw his own conclusion. If he sticks to the idea that he can still control his drinking, tell him that possibly he can - if he is not too alcoholic. But insist that if he is severely afflicted, there may be little chance he can recover by himself.

(92:2) Continue to speak of alcoholism as an illness, a fatal malady. Talk about the conditions of body and mind which accompany it. Keep his attention focused mainly on your personal experience. Explain that many are doomed who never realize their predicament. Doctors are rightly loath to tell alcoholic patients the whole story unless it will serve some good purpose. But you may talk to him about the hopelessness of alcoholism because you offer a solution. You will soon have your friend admitting he has many, if not all, of the traits of the alcoholic. If his own

116

doctor is willing to tell him that he is alcoholic, so much the better. Even though your protégé may not have entirely admitted his condition, he has become very curious to know how you got well. Let him ask you that question, if he will. Tell him exactly what happened to you. Stress the spiritual feature freely. If the man be agnostic or atheist, make it emphatic that he does not have to agree with your conception of God. He can choose any conception he likes, provided it makes sense to him. The main thing is that he be willing to believe in a Power greater than himself and that he live by spiritual principles.

(94:1) Outline the program of action, explaining how you made a self-appraisal, how you straightened out your past and why you are now endeavoring to be helpful to him. It is important for him to realize that your attempt to pass this on to him plays a vital part in your own recovery. Actually, he may be helping you more than you are helping him. Make it plain he is under no obligation to you, that you hope only that he will try to help other alcoholics when he escapes his own difficulties. Suggest how important it is that he place the welfare of other people ahead of his own. Make it clear that he is not under pressure, that he needn't see you again if he doesn't want to. You should not be offended if he wants to call it off, for he has helped you more than you have helped him. If your talk has been sane, quiet and full of human understanding, you have perhaps made a friend. Maybe you have disturbed him about the question of alcoholism. This is all to the good. The more hopeless he feels, the better. He will be more likely to follow your suggestions.

(94:2) Your candidate may give reasons why he need not follow all of the program. He may rebel at the thought of a drastic housecleaning which requires discussion with other people. Do not contradict such views. Tell him you once felt as he does, but you doubt whether you would

117

have made much progress had you not taken action. On your first visit tell him about the Fellowship of Alcoholics Anonymous. If he shows interest, lend him your copy of this book.

(95:1)   Unless your friend wants to talk further about himself, do not wear out your welcome. Give him a chance to think it over. If you do stay, let him steer the conversation in any direction he likes. Sometimes a new man is anxious to proceed at once. And you may be tempted to let him do so. This is sometimes a mistake. If he has trouble later, he is likely to say you rushed him. You will be most successful with alcoholics if you do not exhibit any passion for crusade or reform. Never talk down to an alcoholic from any moral or spiritual hilltop; simply lay out the kit of spiritual tools for his inspection. Show him how they worked with you. Offer him friendship and fellowship. Tell him that if he wants to get well you will do anything to help.

(95:4)   If he thinks he can do the job in some other way, or prefers some other spiritual approach, encourage him to follow his own conscience. We have no monopoly on God; we merely have an approach that worked with us. But point out that we alcoholics have much in common and that you would like, in any case, to be friendly. Let it go at that.

(96:1)   Do not be discouraged if your prospect does not respond at once. Search out another alcoholic and try again. You are sure to find someone desperate enough to accept with eagerness what you offer. We find it a waste of time to keep chasing a man who cannot or will not work with you. If you leave such a person alone, he may soon become convinced that he cannot recover by himself. To spend too much time on any one situation is to deny some other alcoholic an opportunity to live and be happy. One of our Fellowship failed entirely with his first half dozen prospects. He often says that if he had continued to

118

work on them, he might have deprived many others, who have since recovered, of their chance.

(96:2) Suppose now you are making your second visit to a man. He has read this volume and says he is prepared to go through with the Twelve Steps of the program of recovery. Having had the experience yourself, you can give him much practical advice. Let him know you are available if he wishes to make a decision and tell his story, but do not insist upon it if he prefers to consult someone else.

(96:3) He may be broke and homeless. If he is, you might try to help him about getting a job, or give him a little financial assistance. But you should not deprive your family or creditors of money they should have. Perhaps you will want to take the man into your home for a few days. But be sure you use discretion. Be certain he will be welcomed by your family, and that he is not trying to impose upon you for money, connections, or shelter. Permit that and you only harm him. You will be making it possible for him to be insincere.

(97:0) You may be aiding in his destruction rather than his recovery.

(97:1) Never avoid these responsibilities, but be sure you are doing the right thing if you assume them. Helping others is the foundation stone of your recovery. A kindly act once in a while isn't enough. You have to act the Good Samaritan every day, if need be. It may mean the loss of many nights' sleep, great interference with your pleasures, interruptions to your business. It may mean sharing your money and your home, counseling frantic wives and relatives, innumerable trips to police courts, sanitariums, hospitals, jails and asylums. Your telephone may jangle at any time of the day or night. Your wife may sometimes say she is neglected. A drunk may smash the furniture in your home, or burn a mattress. You may have to fight with him if he is violent. Sometimes you will have to call a doctor and administer sedatives under his direction. Another time you may have to send for the police or an ambulance. Occasionally you will have to meet such conditions.

(97:4) For the type of alcoholic who is able and willing to get well, little charity, in the ordinary sense of the word, is needed or wanted. The men who cry for money and shelter before conquering alcohol, are on the wrong track. Yet we do go to great extremes to provide each other with these very things, when such action is warranted. This may seem inconsistent, but we think it is not.

(98:1) It is not the matter of giving that is in question, but when and how to give. That often makes the difference between failure and success. The minute we put our work on a service plane, the alcoholic commences to rely upon our assistance rather than upon God. He clamors for this or that, claiming he cannot master alcohol until his material needs are cared for. Nonsense. Some of us have taken very hard knocks to learn this truth: Job or no job - wife or no wife - we simply do not stop drinking so long as we place dependence upon other people ahead of dependence on God.

(98:2) Burn the idea into the consciousness of every man that he can get well regardless of anyone. **The only condition is that he trust in God and clean house.**

(102:2) Your job now is to be at the place where you may be of maximum helpfulness to others, so never hesitate to go anywhere if you can be helpful. You should not hesitate to visit the most sordid spot on earth on such an errand. Keep on the firing line of life with these motives and God will keep you unharmed.

(163:4) So our fellow worker will soon have friends galore. Some of them may sink and perhaps never get up, but if our experience is a criterion, more than half of those approached will become fellows of Alcoholics Anonymous. When a few men in this city have found themselves, and have discovered the joy of helping others to face life again, there will be no stopping until everyone in that town has had his opportunity to recover - if he can and will.

(164:1) Still you may say: "But I will not have the benefit of contact with you who write this book." We cannot be sure. God will determine that, so you must remember that your real reliance is always upon Him. He will show you how to create the fellowship you crave.

(164:2) Our book is meant to be suggestive only. We realize we know only a little. God will constantly disclose more to you and to us. Ask Him in your morning meditation what you can do each day for the man who is still sick. The answers will come, if your own house is in order. But obviously you cannot transmit something you haven't got. See to it that your relationship with Him is right, and great events will come to pass for you and countless others. This is the Great Fact for us.

(164:3) Abandon yourself to God as you understand God. Admit your faults to Him and to your fellows. Clear away the wreckage of your past. Give freely of what you find and join us. We shall be with you in the Fellowship of the Spirit, and you will surely meet some of us as you trudge the Road of Happy Destiny.

(164:4) May God bless you and keep you – until then.

If you have sincerely taken the previous eleven steps to the best of your ability, step 12 states that you have had a spiritual awakening as a direct result of taking the first eleven steps. You have now made yourself fit to be of service to God and those about you. We express our spiritual awakening on a daily basis by practicing the principles of unselfishness, honesty, purity (integrity) and love in all of our affairs.

How does this "spiritual awakening" manifest in our lives?

Most importantly, we are not drinking. We have found the spiritual solution to our drinking problem. Many of us are now aware of a new "God consciousness". Our thoughts are more loving, honest, tolerant and kind. We are more peaceful with others and ourselves. These are all attributes of a spiritual awakening.

A caution from page 85 in The Big Book:

"It is easy to let up on the spiritual program of action (the steps) and rest on our laurels. We are, headed for trouble if we do, for alcohol is a subtle foe. We are not cured of alcoholism. What we have is a daily reprieve contingent on the maintenance of our spiritual condition. Every day is a day we must carry the vision of God's will for us into all of our activities".

And again from page 89 in The Big Book:

"Practical experience shows that nothing will so much insure *IMMUNITY FROM DRINKING* as will intensive work with other alcoholics. It works when all others fail. This is our twelfth suggestion: *Carry this message to other alcoholics!"*

~ ~ ~

Taking Step 12: (the group stands and individually answers)

Will you carry this message to other alcoholics, and practice these principles in all your affairs?

If you answer yes, you have begun taking Step 12.

~ ~ ~

Workshop Close

Congratulations on taking all 12 Steps as presented in our textbook!

These are the steps as presented in The Big Book as AA's ONLY "suggested" program of recovery from the disease of alcoholism. The steps are suggested in the sense that if you do not want to be hit by a train, it is suggested to not play on train tracks.

Complicating the steps in any way does a dis-service to the program, to those who carried this message before us, and to the still suffering alcoholic you will be attempting to help.

As has been seen, there is no writing involved in any of the steps except for the 4th and 10th steps, and these are simple lists.

Do not analyze The Big Book. The Big Book is a set of 12 simple steps leading directly to the spiritual solution to alcoholism.

There is no benefit to creating any other method of taking the steps. It will likely complicate a simple program making recovery more difficult for yourself and for the people you are trying to help.

Simply follow the instructions as they are presented and you will stay sober.

The Big Book has been written in an effective and straightforward way so that we can actually recover, not study recovery, and not become bogged down in psychological exercise, which as Dr. Silkworth points out in The Doctors Opinion, has little effectiveness for helping the alcoholic achieve and maintain sobriety.

By taking all twelve steps, we have now made ourselves fit to be of service to God and those about us. What this means primarily is that it is now our responsibility to sponsor others through these same steps. In fact, our primary role as sponsors is to take our sponsees through these steps as soon as possible.

Once we have taken a sponsee through the steps, we then support them by keeping them focused on sobriety. As sponsors we do this by encouraging our sponsees to continue with personal inventory and daily prayer and meditation, and to continue to help other alcoholics by guiding them through the 12 Steps. If we do this we are doing all we can and all we should to carry this message to other alcoholics. And most importantly of all, we will stay sober.

Essentially, we sponsor others to be sponsors.

Finally, please heed the words of our co-founder Dr. Bob Smith given in his final speech shortly before he died:

"But there are two or three things that flashed into my mind on which it would be fitting to lay a little emphasis; one is the simplicity of our Program. Let's not louse it all up with Freudian complexes and things that are interesting to the scientific mind, but have very little to do with our actual AA work. Our 12 Steps, when simmered down to the last, resolve themselves into the words love and service. We understand what love is and we understand what service is. So let's bear those two things in mind.

"Let us also remember to guard that erring member - the tongue, and if we must use it, let's use it with kindness and consideration and tolerance."

"And one more thing; none of us would be here today if somebody hadn't taken time to explain things to us, to give us a little pat on the back, to take us to a meeting or two, to have done numerous little kind and thoughtful acts in our behalf. So let us never get the degree of smug complacency so that we're not willing to extend or attempt to, that help which has been so beneficial to us, to our less fortunate brothers. Thank you very much."

With deep gratitude to the spiritual solution to our drinking problem, we have been given the gift of life. More importantly, we have been given the gift of life with a purpose. That purpose is to serve others. Use it wisely.

Stay sober - Take the steps

Take another alcoholic through the steps

Peace and sobriety to you all

End Of Workshop

~ ~ ~ ~ ~

Part 3
Practicing These Principles

Steps 10, 11, and 12 - The Maintenance Steps

Practicing These Principles In All Our Affairs

Steps 10, 11 and 12 are the "maintenance" steps, the steps we take or practice on a daily basis if we are truly "practicing these principles in all our affairs." Just attending AA meetings, avoiding drinking and drugging, and dropping our most egregious character defects, is not practicing AA principles.

It is by continuing to take personal inventory, continuing with a daily prayer and meditation practice and continuing to help other alcoholics, that we continue to grow along spiritual lines and keep ourselves fit to be of service to God and those about us. By practicing steps 10, 11 and 12 we are exercising our new-found spiritual muscles.

Many of us have heard the phrase "living in the first three steps." What does this mean? It means that we have conceded that we were alcoholic, that we believe or are willing to believe in a higher power, and that we may have turned our will and our life over to the care of our higher power.

Many alcoholics who practice only the first three steps drink again. They are only practicing twenty-five percent of the 12 Steps and have never addressed their self-centered character defects or discovered what a higher power's will is for them. Step 3 is nothing more than a decision to turn our will and our life over to a higher power. Once we do so, we need the remaining steps to develop an understanding of a higher power and to know God's will for us. Without personal inventory, daily prayer and meditation, and being of service to others, we are simply stuck in a nebulous self-centered state with no clear path of recovery.

By practicing step 10, we will know where we are continuing to act selfishly, trying to live by our own will, and we will recognize when we are acting in accordance with our higher powers' will for us. How do we know when we are still acting out of self-will? To the extent that we are resentful, fearful, selfish, dishonest, prideful, jealous, envious or lazy we are still acting in a self-centered manner.

When we are forgiving, loving, honest, humble, trusting, content and taking actions based on these attributes, we can be certain that we are acting in accordance with a higher powers' will for us.

By continuing to take personal inventory, any remaining self-centered defects of character will become apparent. We will avoid the alcoholic's uncanny and dangerous ability to remain blind to self-centered character defects. If we cause harm, we immediately make amends. Through continuing to practice step 11, we humbly ask our higher power to relieve us (of our defects) while we simultaneously strive to strengthen our character assets. This is essential in order to continue to grow along spiritual lines.

By incorporating prayer and meditation into our lives on a daily basis, we will be cultivating our awareness of the presence of our higher power. Increasingly, our thinking will reflect God's will for us. Increasingly, we will be able to clearly see the next right course of action. Steps 10, 11, and 12 are how we keep in fit spiritual condition, and how we deepen our spiritual awakening. This is how we will know for certain what God's will for us is.

We have already used a few prayers to arrive at this point in our recovery. What are we praying for as part of our daily practice? We pray for the knowledge of God's will for us, and the power to carry that out. If we are stuck in a pattern of self-will, we pray for further relief from the bondage of self.

In prayer, we acknowledge our deep gratitude for this simple and very effective program of relieving our alcoholism and deepening our awareness of a spiritual way of life. We ask that the means to recovery through service to others be provided to us.

The second part of step 11, meditation, is essential in developing and maintaining our conscious contact with our higher power. Most religions and spiritual philosophies encourage meditation as a part of spiritual practice. Meditation is how we have a direct experience of being in the presence of our higher power, however we define this higher power. We achieve this by utilizing a method of meditation that enables us to let go of self-centered or ego-centered thoughts and quietly become aware of a higher power's presence within us.

"Our thought-life will be placed on a much higher plane when our thinking is cleared of wrong motives." (page 86, paragraph 3, last sentence, The Big Book)

A very simple and effective method of meditation, one that is used in The Spiritual Solution workshops, is to sit comfortably and quietly and to become aware of the sensation of breathing. As thoughts arise, acknowledge the thoughts and simply let the thoughts go, put them aside. Put thoughts aside and bring your awareness back to the sensation of breathing. As best as you can, do not follow a thought with another thought. Remain disconnected from thoughts and connected to your breath.

Meditation is a practice of ease and joy. It is best not to attempt to force yourself to stop thinking. This is impossible. Simply keep awareness of your breath for as long as possible, and when you notice you are following a thought, let the thought go and return awareness to the sensation of breathing.

Developing a meditation practice takes time and it is best to go slowly. If possible, set aside a place in your home that is clean and clutter-free, even a corner of a room. Use a cushion or pillow to sit on, or a chair if sitting on the floor is uncomfortable. Darken the room and sit quietly as described above. Begin by sitting for a few minutes a day, twice a day, and gradually increase the time devoted to meditation to fifteen or twenty minutes twice a day.

One of the most important thoughts to let go of in meditation are negative judgments about your meditation practice itself. If you are sitting, letting go of thoughts as they arise, and keeping your awareness on your breathing as best you can, you are meditating. Remember, meditation is a practice of ease and joy. Do not burden yourself and your practice with harsh judgments of yourself and unrealistic expectations. Sit quietly, put aside thoughts, and focus on your breath.

The Big Book advises us to continue to develop our spiritual practice by seeking out (reputable and effective) teachers and reading about the many methods of prayer and meditation. Continuing to grow along spiritual lines is an essential and wonderfully rewarding and exciting aspect of recovery that is completely missed by just not drinking and going to meetings. By continuing to develop a prayer and meditation practice, you are taking step 11 on a daily basis.

It is important to remember that neither of our co-founders could stay sober until they included helping other alcoholics achieve sobriety as part of their own sobriety. Dr. Bob was a member of the Oxford Group, a spiritually based group whose method of practice was the inspiration for the 12 Steps. Despite Dr. Bob's commitment to these spiritual principles, he could not stay sober. It was not until his meeting with Bill Wilson that he was able to find a way to finally achieve sobriety. Bill told Bob about the need for an admission of the problem, (that Bob was an alcoholic) a personal inventory, conscious contact with a higher power, and the absolute necessity to help other alcoholics achieve the same spiritual solution to their alcoholism.

Once they included this key element of comfortable, contented, permanent sobriety - helping alcoholics by taking them through the steps, both Bill and Bob were able to finally stay sober. After they experienced their complete psychic change and spiritual awakening, began helping alcoholics take the steps, and practiced these principles in ALL their affairs, (steps 10, 11 and 12) these once hopeless alcoholics never drank again.

What is step 12 telling us to do with the instruction..."carry this message to other alcoholics"?

It is included in step 12 immediately after the declaration that we have had a spiritual awakening as a result of taking the previous 11 steps. We now know that we are fit to carry the same message that Ebby Thacher presented to Bill Wilson, who presented it to Dr. Bob Smith, and now to us. The simple, straightforward message is that we recover in AA by taking the 12 Steps and then by taking others through the 12 Steps. There is no other "suggested" program of recovery offered in Alcoholics Anonymous.

The great realization that our founders and other early members had was that by following this simple program without embellishment, they could stay sober and actually help other alcoholics to stay sober as well.

To re-state a most important point from page 85 in The Big Book:

"It is easy to let up on the spiritual program of action (the steps) and rest on our laurels. We are, headed for trouble if we do, for alcohol is a subtle foe. We are not cured of alcoholism. What we have is a daily reprieve contingent on the maintenance of our spiritual condition. Every day is a day we must carry the vision of God's will for us into all of our activities."

And again from page 89 in The Big Book:

"Practical experience shows that nothing will so much insure *IMMUNITY FROM DRINKING* as will intensive work with other alcoholics. It works when all others fail. This is our twelfth suggestion: *Carry this message to other alcoholics!*"

133

Sponsorship

As sponsors, the most important message we can offer the newcomer is that the AA program of recovery is the 12 Steps as presented in The Big Book. It is of paramount importance, truly with most alcoholics a matter of life and death, that we as sponsors carry a simple, clear and effective message.

We do not assume the role of amateur psychologist, social worker, therapist or counselor. When we take on roles other than the only role we are qualified to assume – sharing recovery through the 12 Steps, we risk confusing our sponsee and making recovery in AA something it was never intended to be, a program of recovery relying on human power rather than a higher power.

We do not create dependent relationships with our sponsees. We need to impress on our sponsees that they are reliant on a higher or greater than human power to relieve their alcoholism. Relying on one's "network" or one's home group to relieve their alcoholism is also relying on human power.

While we offer a patient and loving presence when our sponsees want to discuss their problems or grievances, we wisely and compassionately remind the sponsee that sobriety is not contingent on the elimination of problems. Relief from our self-centered problems is achieved through personal inventory by identifying our part in our upsets, asking in prayer and meditation to be relieved of this bondage of self, and continued service to others.

By continually acting as counselors and therapists, we confuse our sponsees regarding how recovery through the 12 Steps is actually achieved. Our role as AA sponsors is to present the spiritual solution to alcoholism, not a human intervention into the alcoholics' problems of the day. We are then presenting the confusing and discouraging message that recovery in AA is based on problem resolution and participating in meeting after meeting of group therapy hoping to find a human solution to our unique problems. This simply leads the suffering self-centered alcoholic to even more self-centered suffering and not the liberation and freedom found in the 12 Steps.

The only message we are qualified to carry as AA members is that the spiritual solution to alcoholism is found in the 12 Steps. The spiritual solution is the solution to our common problem, alcoholism. Our role as AA sponsors is to take our sponsees through the steps as presented in The Big Book and then encourage them to do the same with others.

We sponsor people to become sponsors. Once we have taken a sponsee through the steps, our role as sponsor is limited. From then on we encourage our sponsees to continue with their personal inventories, continue with their prayer and meditation practice, and to continue to help other alcoholics by guiding them through the 12 Steps. This is exactly how AA began and hopefully how it will continue.

From page 98 in The Big Book "Burn the idea into the consciousness of every man that he can get well regardless of **anyone.** The ONLY condition is that he trust in God and clean house."

What does The Big Book teach regarding sponsorship? In Bill's story we learn that Ebby, Bill's sponsor, explained to Bill the spiritual solution to his (Ebby's) alcoholism he gained from his association with the Oxford Group, in effect taking Bill through the steps, and then impressing on Bill the need to help others.

Ebby is not mentioned again, as his role as Bill's sponsor was over. We then learn of how Bill took the same approach with Dr. Bob Smith, taking him through the steps as they were then, presenting the spiritual solution to Dr. Bob's alcoholism, and then impressing on Bob the need to carry the same message to other alcoholics. Bill's role as Dr. Bob's sponsor was now complete and they both spent the rest of their lives concerned only with how to best carry the spiritual solution to all who would have it.

Dr. Bob died sober after fifteen years of sobriety, and it is estimated that he sponsored over 5000 men and women during this time. Obviously Bob did not spend years, months, or even weeks with his sponsees taking them through the steps. He took them through the steps (most while they were still in a hospital) in one sitting. Dr. Bob then encouraged those he had just taken through the steps to do the same with still-suffering alcoholics in order to stay sober.

The 12th step directs us that once we have had a spiritual awakening as a result of taking the previous 11 steps to then carry the same message to other alcoholics and to practice the principles of recovery in all our affairs.

The Big Book authors are perfectly clear as to what we need to do to stay sober and help other alcoholics: take the 12 Steps to fit ourselves to be of service to God and those about us, and present the same 12 Steps to others. No other "suggestions" are offered, as no other actions can be as effective in helping other alcoholics achieve sobriety.

Dr. Bob offered us much guidance for our interactions with newcomers and each other as members of AA, words spoken as part of his last speech:

> "Let us also remember to guard that erring member - the tongue, and if we must use it, let's use it with kindness and consideration and tolerance. And one more thing; none of us would be here today if somebody hadn't taken time to explain things to us, to give us a little pat on the back, to take us to a meeting or two, to have done numerous little kind and thoughtful acts in our behalf. So let us never get the degree of smug complacency so that we're not willing to extend or attempt to, that help which has been so beneficial to us, to our less fortunate brothers. Thank you."

Nowhere in the Big Book do we read of the extremely complex relationships many current-day sponsors form with their sponsees. When sponsors do more than carry the message of recovery through the 12 Steps, they risk confusing their sponsees' understanding as to what recovery based on spiritual principles actually is. When sponsors take on a larger or more complicated role than what is shown in The Big Book, the sponsor is introducing human power ahead of a higher power.

As sponsors, we take our sponsees through the steps and as members of AA, we are compassionate, helpful and understanding to the newcomer. How we interact with others inside and outside of AA, what our true roles are, will be much more clear and much less complex, once we have fit ourselves through the 12 Steps and are acting in accordance with a higher power's will for us.

As sponsors, or simply as AA members, we may be asked to provide rides to meetings. We may be called from time to time to offer some emotional support to a newcomer or other AA member. These are all part of the "numerous little kind and thoughtful acts" Dr. Bob speaks of. We are very careful not to create dependent relationships with our sponsees or other members. As sponsors, we always encourage our sponsees to rely on a higher power, not human power. As we continue to grow along spiritual lines, we will know when an action is in accordance with God's will and when we are acting out of self-centeredness.

It is also important to let the newcomer know why we attend meetings. As AA members who have fit themselves through the 12 Steps, this is best done by example. We attend meetings to share our experience of recovery through the 12 Steps, the strength we receive from a higher power, and our sincere hope to be of service to other alcoholics by guiding them through the 12 Steps.

We encourage newcomers, as soon as they begin attending meetings, to let others know they are newly sober, to share their own experience of taking the 12 Steps, the new-found power they have received from their higher power, and their sincere desire to help other alcoholics. We explain to our sponsees that their problems with the people and events of their day are addressed in personal inventory and in daily prayer and meditation.

Most importantly, we explain that the most effective and immediate answer to the problems of each day, the most effective and immediate way to relieve the bondage of self-centeredness so characteristic of the alcoholic, is to help another alcoholic.

It is vitally important for new sponsees to learn the role of the sponsor. Sponsors take their sponsees through the steps and then encourage the sponsee to do likewise. We do not "louse it all up with Freudian complexes and things that are interesting to the scientific mind, but have **very little to do with our actual AA work.**" We "explain things" and offer "that help which has been so beneficial to us", the 12 Steps.

Sponsors are not necessarily their sponsee's best friend, although true friendship based on spiritual principles often develops. Sponsors are not shopping companions, gossip partners, poker buddies, taxi drivers, etc. As mentioned elsewhere, sponsors are not counselors or therapists of any kind.

An AA sponsors' role is to first fit themselves by taking the steps as presented in The Big Book and then take sponsees through the steps the same way.

A newcomer must find a qualified sponsor who has fit themselves to take them through the steps. Perhaps the most important question a newcomer can ask of someone they are considering to be their sponsor is **"have you taken the steps as presented in The Big Book, and if you have, will you take me through the steps the same way?"**

If the newcomer receives a 'yes' to BOTH questions, they can be certain they will be given every chance to recover. If either answer is 'no', the newcomer would do best to keep looking for a qualified sponsor.

The Home Group

As important as qualified sponsors are, we all need an effective and focused home group as well. Bill Wilson gave us clear direction regarding the purpose of a home group in a February 1958 Grapevine article. In this article Bill states:

"Sobriety, freedom from alcohol, through the teaching and practice of the 12 Steps is the SOLE purpose of an AA group. Groups have repeatedly tried other activities, and they always failed. If we don't stick to these principles, we shall almost surely collapse. And if we collapse, we cannot help anyone."

The Sole purpose of an AA group is the teaching and practice of the 12 Steps. Many groups do try other activities other than the teaching and practice of the 12 Steps. With a 5% to 7% recovery rate today, AA is on the edge of collapse.

The AA group is where most newcomers first encounter the AA program of recovery. The members of any particular group are responsible for making certain that they are presenting to the newcomer a clear message that recovery through the 12 Steps is the only program of recovery presented by AA. As stated in How It Works, "Here are the steps WE TOOK, which are suggested as a program of recovery."

Each group when taking a group inventory should examine whether the activities of the group are actually the teaching and practice of the 12 Steps.

Do we hold meetings where the newcomer or those still suffering from active alcoholism feel safe and welcome? Are qualified sponsors available to those seeking assistance in their sobriety? Do we let newcomers know that we want to hear what they have to say, or do we arrogantly insist that they "take the cotton out of their ears and put it in their mouths"? Do we hand sick newcomers a list of strangers' phone numbers and tell them that it is their responsibility to call rather than take the newcomer's number and make a few calls ourselves? If a newcomer has a question regarding the AA program of recovery, do we dismiss them by telling them to "keep coming," or do we take the time to explain our program to them?

If our co-founders expressed this kind of arrogance, none of us would be here. Our co-founders actively engaged suffering alcoholics, listening to their questions and concerns and presenting the spiritual solution to alcoholism.

We certainly are not at AA meetings to talk about our problems or grievances of the day or to express false humility (arrogance) by saying we are still as "messed up" as we were when we came into AA x number of years ago, but at least we are not drinking. What hope does this offer to anyone? Yet, this type of false humility is heard often.

If a member of AA feels that they have nothing to offer as far as recovery is concerned, except for going to meetings and avoiding alcohol, find a qualified sponsor to take you through the steps as presented in The Big Book. It really does work, no matter how long it has been since one took a drink.

AA groups and the meetings they hold should be a place of fellowship, emotional and spiritual support, and real friendship, not as a substitute for the 12 Steps, rather as an expression of our service to each other as a result of having achieved the spiritual solution.

Remember, Bill Wilson also said that meetings are held so that the newcomer might bring his problems regarding the spiritual solution and staying sober in AA. We as sober members attend meetings to patiently and compassionately guide newcomers (and anyone else) towards taking the 12 Steps as presented in The Big Book. At meetings, we let newcomers know our own experiences in achieving comfortable, contented sobriety through the 12 Steps.

Length Of Sobriety And Qualification For Service

Many if not most AA groups have a confusing policy of using length of sobriety as the sole qualification for AA members presenting a message of recovery. This policy directly contradicts our founding principle of sobriety dependent on a higher power and helping other alcoholics achieve sobriety.

Many in AA have turned a blind eye to the most significant part of our history and Bill Wilson's great understanding of the need to help another alcoholic in order to maintain sobriety. Both Bill and Dr. Bob had a spiritually based life, Dr. Bob probably more so than Bill, and neither could stay sober UNTIL they started to carry the message of recovery through the 12 Steps.

Nowhere in AA literature does there exist any other definition of sobriety except what Bill wrote in a 1958 Grapevine article in which he stated; "Sobriety, (is) freedom from alcohol through the teaching and practice of the 12 Steps..." We achieve sobriety through the teaching and practice of the 12 Steps, not by somehow avoiding drinking for some length of time.

Simply avoiding drinking is not the defining characteristic of sobriety in AA. It is first "fitting ourselves to be of service to God and those about us," (page 77, The Big Book) through taking the 12 Steps, and then actually being of service by taking others through the steps. We are also of service to others by sharing our recovery through the 12 Steps at meetings during speaking commitments. Speaking at meetings by qualified members

143

is routinely denied them by these arbitrary policies based on length of sober time, rather than quality of sobriety and an understanding of the 12 Steps based on personal experience.

If an AA member has taken the 12 Steps as presented in The Big Book and has achieved sobriety, they have fit themselves to be of service to God and those about them. In fact, their continued sobriety depends on being of service to other alcoholics.

This is the example given to us by Bill, Dr. Bob and other early members. There is no importance placed on length of sobriety as far as a qualification to be of service to other alcoholics. The only requirement to carry the AA message of the spiritual solution to alcoholism found in the 12 steps is that an AA member actually takes the 12 steps.

Establishing a policy based on an arbitrary length of sobriety as qualification for simply helping other alcoholics is antithetical to the AA program of taking the 12 steps as soon as one comes to AA and then guiding others through the steps. The whole AA philosophy is based on the understanding that in order to stay sober AA members must directly help others to stay sober as well.

Bill Wilson began to seek out other alcoholics to guide through the steps when he was only a few days sober. As soon as Dr. Bob stopped drinking permanently, after his second meeting with Bill, Bob also immediately began helping other alcoholics achieve sobriety by presenting the spiritual principles found in the 12 Steps.

If others had told Bill or Bob that if they did not have 90 days, or 6 months or 1 year of sobriety before they could even consider helping others, both would have drank again and none of us would have a 12 step spiritual solution to our alcoholism.

Yet today, it is the strict policy of almost every AA group, and an unwritten and strongly encouraged policy of

AA in general, that an arbitrary amount of time be imposed on members before they are "allowed" to carry a message of recovery to other alcoholics.

This policy has directly contributed to the extremely low recovery rate in AA today.

The only requirement for helping other alcoholics and paramount to sobriety from the day one encounters AA, is to take the steps as presented in The Big Book and then take others through these steps. Newcomers, once they have "fit themselves to be of service to God and those about them" (page 77 The Big Book) should be encouraged to begin carrying this message of recovery directly by guiding others trough the steps and on speaking commitments. Their sobriety depends on helping others in a very direct way.

It is of much more importance that before someone begins to carry the AA message that they experience the "complete psychic change and spiritual awakening" found only through actually taking the 12 steps from The Big Book. If one has done this in the first week of sobriety, they have fit themselves to be of service to God and those about them. Comfortable, contented, permanent sobriety is contingent on the newcomer having other alcoholics available to help.

If an AA member has not taken the steps as presented in The Big Book, no amount of sober time will fit them to be of service to God and those about them. What message of "experience, strength and hope" could a member present if they have yet to personally experience the only suggested program of recovery?

The greatest barrier that newcomers face when coming to AA is that very rarely is the actual program of recovery clearly explained and a genuine opportunity to carry the message of recovery provided, rather than denied. Most newcomers are told to sit down, shut their mouths and if they are lucky enough to avoid drinking for 90 days, a year, or some other arbitrary amount of time, they will then be judged fit to work with others.

The deciding factor prevalent in AA today as to whether an AA member is capable of actually helping another member is not whether they understand the only program of recovery offered in AA through personal experience, but how long have they avoided drinking.

In the early days of AA, most groups did not allow members to attend general AA meetings UNTIL they had taken the steps. Once the newcomer had taken the steps, very early in sobriety, they were ENCOURAGED to help other alcoholics. The early members of AA new that continued sobriety is contingent on the taking **and** teaching of the 12 steps as soon as one enters AA. It is how early members stayed sober and how AA grew exponentially.

I have kept most of my personal experiences out of this book and a recent event at a local meeting illustrates this point so well that it should be told here:

An announcement was made and a sign-up list was passed around the room from the local AA district asking for volunteers to be "temporary contact" people to meet with alcoholics in treatment or as soon as they left treatment. This is a great idea except the requirements were that the person calling on the newcomer must have at least one year of sobriety. There was no requirement that the temporary contact have any understanding of the 12 steps, just that they had somehow avoided drinking for a year. This excludes those that have fit themselves early in sobriety of actually insuring their sobriety by working with other alcoholics.

An AA member who may only be sober a week but who has taken the steps as presented in The Big Book is far more qualified to be of service to another alcoholic than an AA member who has simply not drank and went to meetings for any amount of time. Yet, the fully qualified

146

member would be denied the opportunity to carry the only message we should be presenting, and the opportunity to further strengthen their own sobriety, simply by a completely misguided notion contrary to basic AA principles.

A policy far more consistent with the AA program of recovery would be that no matter how much time an AA member had, before they could be a temporary contact or take on any other service role including speaking at meetings, they had to first have fit themselves by actually taking the 12 Steps. If they are not fit to carry the AA message as defined by our literature, a policy that they do fit themselves would certainly encourage members to do so.

Any other service qualification is arbitrary and contradictory to AA's own stated purpose of staying sober by helping other alcoholics achieve sobriety. The first paragraph of The Big Book chapter "Working With Others", page 89, clearly states "Practical experience shows that nothing will so much insure immunity from drinking as intensive work with other alcoholics. It works when ALL other activities fail!"

12 pages earlier we are taught that the "purpose of sobriety is to fit ourselves (through taking the 12 Steps) to be of maximum service to God and those about us."

Eager members who have taken the 12 Steps are left with nothing to "insure immunity from drinking" while they wait for some misguided notion of an arbitrary amount of sober time to arrive before they can share their experience, strength and hope. Many drink again while waiting. In addition, many that would benefit from hearing their message never do.

147

Special (Exclusive) Meetings

Meetings catering to "special circumstances" have no place in AA. There is nothing gender, problem, sexual orientation, or age specific about the 12 Steps. There is nothing that cannot be discussed regarding recovery through the 12 Steps at any genuine AA meeting. If one feels that there is something "special" regarding a problem that cannot be resolved by practicing the 12 Steps, the resolution is outside the focus and effectiveness of AA.

AA is the spiritual solution to our COMMON problem, recovery from alcoholism. Special problems and unique situations have nothing to do with our common problem. Taking step one, conceding to our innermost self that we are alcoholic, is what unites us in purpose as a fellowship. It is a vital admission that as far as our disease and our recovery is concerned we are all the same. By insisting on what makes us unique, we separate ourselves from the common solution to alcoholism.

As AA members, it is our responsibility to only present a clear and loving message of recovery that includes all alcoholics who seek the spiritual solution. Predatory, prejudicial and intolerant behavior has absolutely no place in the spiritual setting of an AA meeting. Meetings must have a feeling of safety and welcome to anyone and everyone. All of our lives depend on it. If some feel it necessary to form a new AA group due to the unsatisfactory or intolerant nature of one's present home group, it will serve all members sobriety well to form a group founded on the 12 Steps including the principles of patience, tolerance, kindness, love and service and to include all who seek recovery.

Other Substances and Singleness Of Purpose

One of the great misunderstandings in AA is what is meant by singleness of purpose. Singleness of purpose means that we share one purpose, recovery from alcoholism through the 12 Steps. We are not concerned with solving each other's unique individual problems or emotional upsets. We are in AA to solve our COMMON problem, alcoholism.

Singleness of purpose means that during AA meetings, we have no interest in politics, the environment, religion, sports, or world affairs. We do not introduce psychotherapy at meetings, or exercise programs, or vitamin therapy, or any specific connection to a particular church as a means of recovery. We do not get involved in any other topic that would detract from our primary purpose of staying sober and helping other alcoholics achieve sobriety.

Singleness of purpose does not imply in any way that we never discuss substances other than alcohol and it certainly does not mean that a member also addicted to drugs other than alcohol should be made to feel uncomfortable discussing their use of other drugs.

From the beginning of AA, those with addictions to other substances were welcome in AA and were of utmost importance to the early years of AA. In one of the most referred to stories in The Big Book, "Acceptance Was The Answer", the writer talks of his addiction to Benzedrine, tranquilizers, codeine, Percodan, and intravenous Demerol and morphine. The recovering alcoholic doctor writes:

"Giving up alcohol was not enough for me; I've had to give up all mood and mind affecting chemicals in order to stay sober and comfortable." He also writes "Today I feel I have used up my right to a **chemical** peace of mind."

If a story about a recovering drug addict AND alcoholic is included in The Big Book, should we not be tolerant of those who are also addicted to substances besides alcohol?

Included in this story is one of the most quoted lines from The Big Book, and one of the key components of recovery, "acceptance is the answer to all my problems", yet we often practice just the opposite.

As members of Alcoholics Anonymous, we can encourage greater acceptance of all members by identifying ourselves as alcoholics, rather than calling attention to our individual unique differences.

Great problems have been created for individuals, groups and for AA as a whole, due to the lack of acceptance of members with more than just an addiction to alcohol. Shortsighted misinterpretation of singleness of purpose along with fear and intolerance has forced many out of AA and back to active alcoholism.

Singleness of purpose simply means that we unite around the spiritual solution to alcoholism and keep our message to those that so desperately need it to recovery through the 12 Steps.

As quoted in the preface to this book, from 'A Vision For You' from The Big Book:

"...It became customary to set apart one night a week for a meeting to be **attended by anyone or everyone interested in a spiritual way of life**."

This clearly points to the singleness of purpose of carrying the message of a spiritual way of life to anyone and everyone. Do we really believe that AA will be diminished by offering our 12 step program to people whose addictions are in addition to addiction to the drug alcohol?

We are all aware that as recovered alcoholics, we cannot safely use any mood or mind-altering substance. Yet, if a compulsion to smoke marijuana comes over someone, many groups would refuse him or her the acceptance to voice this at a meeting, (even though taking any type of mood or mind-altering drug would more than likely lead back to alcoholic drinking).

It would be best for us to be more concerned with who we may be of service to, rather than who we should exclude from a fellowship of drunks and ex-drunks. There is hardly a member today that has not tried other substances, and this has been true since our founding.

When our fellowship was just beginning, we were desperate to find other alcoholics to help so that we could stay sober. Fulfilling our primary purpose to stay sober and help other alcoholics achieve sobriety does not mean we exclude people simply because their addiction to alcohol also included addiction to other substances.

One of the points Bill makes in the book The Twelve Steps And Twelve Traditions is that we might reach those that do not have to go as far "down the ladder" as some of us did. If someone's alcoholism has not (yet) developed to some arbitrary point, isn't it best to have them experience the complete psychic change and spiritual awakening found in the 12 Steps, rather than experience years of suffering and possible death? Are we really so tenuous in our own sobriety that we fear helping someone with a similar addiction, if not the exact same addiction? We should be more concerned with losing our true singleness of purpose - of carrying the message of the spiritual solution found in the 12 Steps to those that need it.

The Big Book describes the alcoholics' real purpose (once given the great gift of sobriety) on page 77:

"Our real PURPOSE is to be of maximum service to God and **the people about us.**"

How does it take anything away from AA by including someone who may have been addicted to chemicals other than alcohol, or someone with a need to talk about their use of other substances from time to time?

Today, AA is in far greater danger of completely losing its focus by discussing everything *but* the 12 Steps at many meetings.

This is how we are losing our singleness of purpose and it is precisely this issue that Bill Wilson cautioned all of us as AA members to guard against.

The Meaning Of Conference Approved Literature

There is much misunderstanding about what "Conference approved" means. Many groups and individual members believe that no literature should be displayed at AA meetings or read by AA members unless it is "Conference Approved". As stated below "Conference Approved" literature is simply material "approved" for publication by the General Services Conference and does not imply ANYTHING else.

Long before the existence of AA World Services, The General Service Conference or The General Service Office, AA groups and AA members read whatever inspirational literature they found useful. Dr. Bob and Bill were inspired by Emmet Fox's Sermon On The Mount and many other books, including The Bible, were read at AA meetings.

Keep in mind that the Grapevine is not "conference approved" yet it is sold at many AA meetings, as it should be. There are even "Grapevine" meetings.

Any two or more alcoholics meeting in support of their sobriety is an AA meeting whose sole authority is a loving God expressing itself through the Group's conscience. What reading material that individuals or groups may find useful has no bearing on whether their meeting is a genuine AA meeting.

The General Service Conference's role is not to approve or disapprove individual AA members reading material and does not determine what reading material may be used or sold at meetings.

~~~

(The following is from the General Service Office of

155

Alcoholics Anonymous)
Source: http://www.aa.org/en_pdfs/smf-29_en.pdf
CONFERENCE-APPROVED LITERATURE
Conference-approved" — What It Means to You

"The term "Conference-approved" describes written or audiovisual material approved by the (General Service) Conference for publication by G.S.O. This process assures that everything in such literature is in accord with A.A. principles. Conference-approved material always deals with the recovery program of Alcoholics Anonymous or with information about the A.A. Fellowship.

"The term has no relation to material not published by G.S.O. **It does not imply Conference disapproval of other material about A.A. A great deal of literature helpful to alcoholics is published by others, and A.A. does not try to tell any individual member what he or she may or may not read.**

"Conference approval assures us that a piece of literature represents solid A.A. experience. Any Conference-approved booklet or pamphlet goes through a lengthy and painstaking process, during which a variety of A.A.s from all over the United States and Canada read and express opinions at every stage of production.

"Central offices and intergroups do write and distribute pamphlets or booklets that are not Conference-approved. If such pieces meet the needs of the local membership, they may be legitimately classified as "A.A. literature." There is no conflict between A.A. World Services, Inc. (A.A.W.S. — publishers of Conference-approved literature), and central offices or intergroups — rather they complement each other. The Conference does not disapprove of such material.

"G.S.O. does develop some literature that does not have to be approved by the Conference, such as service material, Guidelines and bulletins."

Reprinted with Permission of A.A. World Services, Inc.

Afterword

Are we, as sober members, doing all we can to carry the message of the 12 Steps to other alcoholics? Have we "fit ourselves to be of service to God and those about us"? Are we carrying the message of recovery through the 12 Steps and not complicating a simple program?

As stated earlier, AA has become diminished to the point where many meetings are nothing more than misguided group therapy and behavior modification sessions. We use terms like "staying connected to my network" rather than striving to carry the true message of recovery based on the 12 Steps. While "staying connected to our network," we share our problems and grievances of the day and encourage others to do the same. Is it any surprise then that this self-centered focus on our problems continues in our meetings?

Rather than take the time to guide a newcomer through the steps, we dismiss them by telling them to "take the slogans." Newcomers are told to not drink and make 90 meetings in 90 days. If an alcoholic could just not drink, they would not be at an AA meeting. Just making meetings is in no way a substitute for taking the 12 Steps. AA does not have any other program of recovery except the recovery achieved by the taking and teaching of the 12 Steps.

At many meetings, while we go around the room and share our problems of the day, no one is offered a program of recovery. Instead, we "identify" with each other's individual problems, which distract us from our common problem, and this simply fuels the next days "networking."

Are we uniting around a singleness of purpose of carrying the message of recovery through the 12 Steps, or are we

157

commiserating by the sharing of problems and grievances? If AA is designed to be the spiritual solution to alcoholism, should we not unite around providing the spiritual solution to all alcoholics?

Perhaps it was easier in the early days of AA when there was no "networking," no cell phones or social media. Folks at meetings were never seen texting, updating their Facebook page, or leaving a meeting to take a cell phone call. We stayed sober by attending a meeting or two a week, being fully present with other alcoholics, and sharing our recovery through the 12 Steps.

Our early members did not have the time or the means to continually discuss and analyze each other's problems. As stated in the AA preamble: "Alcoholics Anonymous is a fellowship of men and women who share their experience, strength and hope with each other to solve their COMMON problem, and help others to recover from alcoholism." Our common problem is alcoholism; all the other problems discussed today are a distraction from solving our common problem.

Recovery through the 12 Steps is not contingent on creating a life free of problems. By taking the 12 Steps and guiding others through the steps, our problems cease being a source of distraction and self-centered preoccupation. We learn that our sobriety is contingent only on our spiritual condition. We do not gain sobriety to wallow in our problems and grievances and then hope to not drink again.

As sponsors or simply as sober members of AA, by continually commiserating with each other's problems, we reinforce the misguided notion that we drink because we have difficult and unique problems, and that by discussing our problems within our network or at meetings, we will somehow achieve the comfortable, contented sobriety promised only by taking the 12 Steps.

This is not to say that we do not provide a loving and compassionate presence to those that are emotionally or spiritually upset. Our response though, (as someone who has recovered through the 12 Steps), should be to direct those in distress to take an inventory in order to discover their part in the upset, to seek their higher power's guidance in prayer, to sit quietly in meditation, and, in order to shift their focus from their own problems, to help another alcoholic.

Our role as sponsors is to take new sponsees through the steps immediately, and then encourage and assist them in taking others through the steps. Once we have taken a newcomer (or any member) through the steps, our primary role as a sponsor is limited. The sponsor/sponsee relationship was never meant to be a lifetime commitment and sponsors were never meant to be their sponsees personal therapist or daily confessor.

By actually practicing steps 10, 11 and 12 on a daily basis, we will know how to "intuitively handle situations which used to baffle us" and we will "know a new peace, and a new freedom" as our awareness of our higher power develops. There will be no reason to talk with all those in our "network" about our problems and grievances. We learn to rely on personal inventory, a daily practice of prayer and meditation, and of being of service to others, to maintain true humility and keep in fit spiritual condition.

By relying on our "network" to solve our problems, and by encouraging others to do so, we are attempting to rely on human power instead of our higher power. It does not work and the discouragement and dissatisfaction brought about by this continual airing of problems and grievances will lead many back to drinking.

As stated earlier, by Bill Wilson, "The teaching and practice of the 12 Steps is the SOLE purpose of an AA group."

What is the sole purpose of most AA groups today? If it is not the teaching and practice of the 12 Steps, what message is the newcomer receiving? All of the many activities that we do as AA members, making coffee, chairing meetings, speaking, setting up and cleaning up meetings, taking on service positions, are all vitally important to our group and AA as a whole, but none of these are a substitute for carrying the message of recovery through the 12 Steps.

If you want comfortable contented sobriety, if you want the spiritual solution to alcoholism, take the steps. If you want others to have comfortable, contented sobriety, share the spiritual solution with them by taking them through the steps.

Many members today have fit themselves to be of service as described in The Big Book. AA would not have survived without them. Hopefully, we will regain our singleness of purpose as a fellowship of alcoholics who have found recovery through the 12 Steps and are now fit to guide others who are still suffering.

Our primary purpose is to stay sober and help other alcoholics achieve sobriety. If we fit ourselves through taking the 12 Steps as presented in the Big Book and then help other alcoholics achieve sobriety, permanent sobriety is virtually guaranteed. (See The Big Book, page 89, paragraph 1)

By all of us fitting ourselves to be of service to God and those about us through the teaching and practice of the 12 Steps, Alcoholics Anonymous will again become an effective program of recovery and regain the momentum it once had, which led to tremendous growth and its ability to save the lives of all alcoholics seeking the spiritual solution to their alcoholism.

The great majority of alcoholics who actually take all 12 Steps as presented in The Big Book, and practice the maintenance steps (steps 10, 11, and 12), including taking others through the steps, never drink again.

It is the author's strong wish and intention that all who read this book will find that the message of recovery presented here will provide the comfortable, contented, useful and permanent sobriety that as alcoholics we all seek. Peace, love, service and sobriety to you all as together we trudge the road of happy destiny.

About The Author

John H was first introduced to AA from a court-imposed treatment center at age 19. He did not take the steps or seek a spiritual solution to his alcoholism and drank (and used) within two weeks of leaving treatment. By the time John reached the age of 25 he had been an around-the-clock drunk for many years, and was close to dying from the effects of alcoholism. He then went to his second treatment center and was re-introduced to AA. After struggling but staying sober for six months, John's second sponsor, Bob H., took John through the steps in the manner described in this book. The obsession to drink was lifted and John experienced a "complete psychic change and spiritual awakening." After 17 years of continuous sobriety, John stopped practicing the simple principles learned by taking the 12 Steps and (most importantly) John stopped helping other alcoholics by taking them through the steps. After nearly 20 years of sobriety, John drank again as the result of his failure to keep himself fit to be of service to God and those about him. He drank for six years, and once again close to death from the effects of alcoholism, a fit AA member, Jim K intervened, and John was blessed to return to AA. Again, John took the steps (as they are presented here) and experienced another "complete psychic change and spiritual awakening." John stays sober with a daily practice of inventory, prayer and meditation, and service to others, primarily guiding other alcoholics in taking and teaching the 12 Steps.

Contact and Workshop Information

John and his partner, Moira K, lead *The Spiritual Solution 1-Day 12 Step Workshops* in New Jersey and Pennsylvania, and elsewhere upon request. Upcoming workshops are listed at www.thespiritualsolution.com and
www.johnh12steps.com

John maintains a recovery and 12 Steps blog at www.johnh12steps.com

John also teaches meditation classes at the *The Cross River Meditation Center* and maintains a blog related to his meditation center and spiritual practice at:
www.simpleenlightenment.org

John can be contacted via email at
ssbook@johnh12steps.com and johnh12steps@gmail.com

To buy additional copies of this book, please visit
www.amazon.com or www.johnh12steps.com

Workshop handouts and 4th Step inventory checklists are available for free download at www.johnh12steps.com.

Made in the USA
San Bernardino, CA
25 May 2020